JACQUES STAEHLE

The
ENERGY
That
HEALS

The Complete
Acupressure Guide

THE ENERGY THAT HEALS
Jacques Staehle

This edition published in Great Britain MCMXCV *by Carnell plc,*
28 Eccleston Square, London SW1V 1PU.

Copyright © MCMXCV *Editions Reuille, Switzerland.*

Typeset by SJ Design and Publishing, Bromley, Kent.

Printed by Clays Ltd, St Ives plc.

ISBN 1-85779-745-0

Table of Contents

Foreword

I have wanted to publish this book for a long time. Indeed, I have always seen the human body as a very special entity that is both simple and complex. Extraordinary beauty mingled with an impression of mystery.

I talked it over with Jacques Staehle and he was surprised by my comments. For him, the energy that runs through our body is every bit as real as the skin that covers it.

Ever since the dawn of time, the Chinese have known how to materialise this energy. Their traditions teach them that the human body is woven from threads of energy and that often, with the pressure exerted by just one finger, one can increase or decrease the flow of this vital energy.

I knew of Jacques Staehle's work. I attended, then organised, all his seminars in Switzerland. Every time, he met with the same success, the same magic.

He offered me a practical, well-illustrated and complete work. A work of synthesis which shows, explains and guides you to the final result.

You now have this book in your hands. It is undoubtedly one of the best works we have ever published.

I know it will be of great service to you and your loved ones. Don't hesitate to recommend it to other people.

With just one finger, you will soon be able to work miracles.

With my best wishes for good health.

Jean-Claude Reuille
Publisher

ABOUT THE AUTHOR

Jacques Staehle, formerly adviser and scientific director of the World Natural Medicines Association, is an acupuncturist, physiotherapist and naturopath. Before writing more than 21 books on health, Jacques Staehle himself suffered serious health problems. He turned to yoga and discovered the way to a better lifestyle, then decided to perfect his knowledge in the fields of nutritional hygiene, the use of plants and plant aromas, before finally learning the technique of acupressure. He is the author of the following books, among others:

Aromas and Energy, Chakras and Energy, Get rid of Pain, Flatten your Stomach, Guide to Sexual Enjoyment, Practical Guide to Natural Beauty, and *The Gentle Way to Good Health.*

CHAPTER 1

Introduction

Explaining acupressure

Acupressure can be considered as the art of living in perfect health thanks to the stimulation of energy points in the body. Indeed, it is quite possible to stimulate energy points in the body by massaging them with the fingertip: this is acupressure; if needles are used, it is called Acupuncture or, even better, using an electronic device, this is called Electro-Puncture.

The purpose and potential of acupressure

The stimulation of energy points allows us to harmonise our energy by regulating its circulation within the body.

Fast relief is often obtained from pain, whether the pain is in the joints or muscles or due to rheumatism, injury, digestion, nerves, the weather or even psychological. The same applies to most functional disorders.

Acupressure easily solves these little problems that trouble our daily lives, but it also gives excellent results when used to treat long-standing disorders.

The case of the author of this book confirms the effectiveness of this technique. *"I had suffered from back pain for 18 years when I discovered Chinese acupressure and its curative methods. After having applied this technique to certain points appropriate to my condition, I was at last able to rid myself of this pain which, until then, was only relieved by using painkillers."*

Although it is not a universal cure, acupressure has proved just as effective for thousands of other people who have recovered their joy in life, as a result of its preventive and curative qualities.

Relieving pain is not the only ill that can be cured by acupressure; it has proved its effectiveness in beauty treatments such as improving the condition of the skin if it is too dry or too greasy, treating bags under the eyes, halting hair loss, getting rid of dandruff...

Acupressure is the art of living in perfect health thanks to the stimulation of specific points that get rid of tiredness and help fight stress and illness. It is an excellent way of avoiding 'flu, tonsillitis or sinusitis. It is also a science involving self-control which allows one to remain calm in all circumstances and to maintain a better balance in one's life.

Acupressure teaches us body language. Thus, we understand that pain is a sort of alarm signal warning us of biological or psychic malfunctions. All we have to do is take heed of this warning and regulate our body systems by stimulating specific points, following a healthy diet and using plants and their aromatic essential oils. One can, therefore, say that by eliminating pain, acupressure also treats its cause and prevents us from suffering certain illnesses.

Studying genuine acupressure will change your life

Not only will you be rid of much discomfort and possibly illness but you will also have a better understanding of life. You will find answers to many questions such as: Why is the heart symbolic of love? Why do we say we 'have a heavy heart'? Or even a 'heart of gold'? You won't be surprised to discover that there are points on the heart meridian that are capable of helping you recover the enjoyment of life you have lost due to an emotional shock. You will also understand why feelings of affection can have such a broad influence on the heartbeat, and then it will become obvious that it is easy to get rid of nervous heart pain simply be stimulating one or two energy points.

Acupressure also explains why we have a preference for certain tastes such as sweet or savoury, spicy or acid, bitter ... why we prefer one colour to another, why we feel better or worse during a certain season, etc. You will learn that everything has a reason for existing, that nothing happens by chance.

Acupressure will help you conquer insomnia, anxiety ... It will also prove an astonishing remedy for reviving someone who has fainted, in the space of just a few seconds.

This book deals with the role of energy and its circulation along the meridians. We'll begin by studying the energy points and then look into how they can be combined.

CHAPTER 2

Basic Principles

The technique of acupressure results from an obvious fact:

Life requires and produces energy.

What is energy?

Matter and energy are so closely dependent on each other that physicists would be tempted to say that matter is nothing more than condensed energy; but energy is – above all – power, resulting from molecular movements that produce heat, a mechanical effect, electricity, chemical reactions causing fireworks – or an atomic bomb – to explode... In other words, energy is the power that produces all dynamic phenomena, for better or for worse...

Did you know that inside the sun, the pressure and the temperature are so high that hydrogen atoms melt together and their explosion liberates heat and light energy through space?

Did you know that if man was able to 'free' all the energy contained in a kilogram of pebbles, sufficient energy would be released to propel a tanker round the world 200 times?

Did you know that solar energy allows plants to fix the carbon dioxide in the air, thus giving them the possibility of manufacturing carbohydrates with the carbon they have retained since, when they decompose, carbohydrates give off carbon dioxide and the energy necessary for maintaining their cellular activity? One could, therefore, say that life is the result of a whole chain of physico-chemical phenomena producing – and requiring – energy.

Human life results from a series of physiological phenomena such as respiration, digestion, blood circulation, etc. All these processes take place thanks to molecules exchanging various particles. Whenever a molecule liberates an element, this element joins another molecule and produces energy.

Such exchanges are fuelled by energy. This is true at all levels. All movement both requires and produces energy.

These energy phenomena are governed by laws that specialists in nuclear physics are beginning to understand. They now acknowledge the analogy between what happens within the human body, which comprises thousands of millions of cells, and the cosmic universe, which comprises thousands of millions of planets. This observation gives rise to a whole new philosophy for which scientists are now beginning to find an explanation (and which, it is hoped, will be covered in another book by the same author).

For the moment, let's keep our feet on the ground and take care of our aches and pains. In most cases, the problem is an energy stoppage which must be cleared by stimulating energy control points. These control points are located along the energy circulation routes known as meridians.

Methods of treatment by acupressure

The purpose of using acupressure is to regulate the circulation of energy and to allow it to be suitably distributed throughout the body. Our physiological, biological and psychic well-being are dependent on these energy phenomena.

An energy overload produced by a distressed organ can cause pain along the corresponding meridian's route, at a specific point or in a whole area. For example, if the gall-bladder has trouble evacuating bile, this will cause an energy overload. This in turn will provoke a migraine attack in which the pain is situated exactly at the departure point of the gall-bladder meridian, ie, at the outer corner of the eye and in the region of the temple. In some cases, this pain will radiate round the side of the head, especially beneath the occipital protuberance at the back of the neck, which is where we find the twentieth gall-bladder point.

To get rid of this migraine, we need to disperse the dispersion point on the Gall-bladder meridian, 38GB, which is on the outer side of the leg. By stimulating this point, the functioning of the gall-bladder and its energy are activated, then the energy overload is dissipated and the migraine disappears of its own accord.

First of all, the migraine is an alarm signal telling us that the gall-bladder is not functioning correctly.

Secondly, by treating the pain, we have also treated its cause.

Now, let's take a look at a completely different case:

This time, we are talking about an energy deficiency, such as tiredness or muscular weakness, for example. The meridians responsible for this deficiency must therefore be tonified, using a certain technique.

In this case, since yang energy is lacking, we must boost it.

If, on the contrary, there is an excess of yang energy, we would have had to disperse it.

To decide whether we need to boost or to disperse a given point, we must first of all understand what yin and yang are all about.

In this book, (-). means 'disperse' and (+). means 'boost', (PM) means Principal Meridian and (EV) means Extraordinary Vessel.

Stimulation of points by acupressure

'Boosting'

In order to boost a point, we press on this point, rotating clockwise, giving impetus in the same direction as the energy flow, for one or two minutes.

'Dispersion'

In order to disperse a point, we press on this point, rotating anticlockwise, giving impetus in the opposite direction to the energy flow, for one or two minutes.

Stimulating points using the *Electronic Pointer* ®

The stimulation of energy points can be made even more effective by using an electronic device: the ELECTRONIC POINTER.

This apparatus detects the precise position of a point and can then immediately stimulate it, either boosting or dispersing the energy flow.

This is a unique device, designed specially to facilitate the location of a point and its immediate stimulation. It is extremely easy to use and completely risk-free since it is powered by a 9-volt battery readily found on the market, which can last for more than a year.

The pointer should be moved across the area in which the required point is situated and a bleep and light will show you exactly where it is. Then, all you have to do is press the button on the underside of the device for fifteen seconds for it to emit a small electronic stimulation. The bleep and the light will show you are in stimulation mode.

Thanks to this apparatus, the technique is easier to use and results appear sooner.

This device can be used on dry, damp as well as normal skins thanks to a detection selector. To boost a point, just place the lever on '+' and stimulate it for 10 to 15 seconds. To disperse a point, just place the lever on '-' and stimulate it for 10 to 15 seconds.

Stimulating both sides

Unless stated otherwise, you must always stimulate points on both sides of the body. All points are bilateral, in other words they exist on the right and on the left side, except for the Conception Vessel and the Governing Vessel which are unilateral, or central. The Conception Vessel runs along the central line down the front of the body and the Governing Vessel follows the rear central line, mainly along the backbone.

Number of sessions necessary

This depends on the disorder being treated.

To stop smoking, one session a day might be necessary, until the desired results are obtained; these could alternate with sessions designed to reduce the subject's appetite or nervousness.

To improve sight, one or two sessions a week; for sciatica, just two or three sessions should suffice.

As a rule, stick to one session a day and as soon as the problem disappears, stop the treatment. If you have to undertake several treatments, start with the most important.

The art of boosting or dispersing – whose purpose is to balance the yin and the yang of our energy and allow us to live in universal harmony – is covered in the next section.

Yin and Yang

To simplify the explanation of yin and yang, we shall use **the sun** as the fundamental example of yang.

The sun produces light and heat.

It encourages dryness and movement.

Water, the main component of living matter (our body contains more than 70% water) cannot move at temperatures below 0 degrees C.

We are also more inclined to travel during the day and even more so in good weather, particularly in summer.

Darkness encourages rest.

Everything external is yang. The sun's rays touch the earth's crust, the skin and everything external. Southern peoples are more outward-going than Northerners.

However, one must always bear in mind the relativity between yin and yang because nothing is absolutely pure; there is always some yin in anything yang and some yang in anything yin. Thus, the skin is yang in relation to muscles, which are yin in relation to the skin but yang in relation to bones. This is why clouds are such a good example for illustrating the relativity of yin. The thicker a cloud, the less we see of the sun's light and the more damp is felt in the atmosphere. All this is yin.

Moreover, an excess of yang can change into yin. For example, when the temperature climbs too high, we no longer want to move but would rather go for a snooze. Another example: when someone becomes too angry, they can become depressed after having exploded. Similarly, an excess of yin can provoke symptoms of an excess of yang, just like extreme cold provokes burns.

YIN (-).	YANG (+).
Cloud	Sun
Darkness	Light
Cold	Heat
Damp (water, blood)	Dryness
Interior	Exteriort
Rest	Movement
Fertilisation	Defence

Excess of YIN (-).	Excess of YANG (+).
Dislike of cold	Dislike of heat
Phobia of the cold	Thermophobia
Excessive diuresis	Insufficient diuresis
(5 times a day)	(3 times a day)
Excessive menstruation	Insufficient menstruation
Extended periods	Amenorrhoea
(more than 5 days)	(absence of menstruation)
Muscular tiredness	Cramp
internalisation	externalisation
Inertia	Exaggerated movement
Lymph (indolence)	Excitability
Inner nervousness	Outer nervousness
Sleepiness	Insomnia
Slowing of functions	Burns
Insensitivity	Inflammation

In cases of an excess of yang, we disperse (-).
In cases of insufficient yang, we boost (+).
We can boost or disperse a meridian, an organ, a function.
We can boost or disperse the whole body.
We can boost or disperse a region of the body.

Simplified table of yin/yang relations

The best way to believe it is to try it!

Here are some examples of situations that frequently poison our lives and which can be resolved almost instantly.

Try putting this fantastic method into practice right now, by stimulating the points which apply to your present condition.

You are highly strung:	Disperse 4LI (p31), 36S (p36) and 3Lv (p82).
You are tired:	Boost 6Sp (p43), 6CV (p131) and 12CV (p132).
You suffer from stomach-ache, diarrhoea, spasms:	Disperse 9Sp (p43).
You have a cough:	Disperse 7L (p27–28).
You are sunburnt:	Disperse 7L (p27–28).

The evolution of yin and yang

Yin and yang are two forces which are opposites and complementary. This duality is constantly present: good and bad, positive and negative, day and night, inside and outside, hot and cold, activity and rest...

But nothing is 100% yin or 100% yang. Everything is mostly yin or mostly yang and proportions vary constantly.

For example, the yin-yang evolution over a period of 24 hours: Midday represents maximum yang. Midnight offers maximum yin.

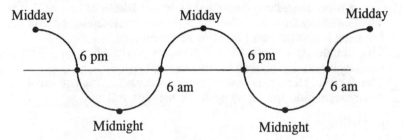

A 24-Hour Cycle

But the yang starts to climb as soon as midnight has passed and continues until midday, when it starts to fall.

This is all very gradual, but also varies with the seasons.

Everything comprises both yin and yang.

Thus, we can say that men are more yang than women but men can be more or less yang and women can be more or less yin. Yin attracts yang and vice versa.

An excessively yang condition (extreme excitement, hysteria) can suddenly become very yin (nervous depression), which sometimes follows on from excessive nervousness.

For materialistic minds, this notion of yin and yang is not always so easy to grasp since it symbolises movement. But what is life, if not an eternal movement of energy, since life cannot exist without molecular movement?

Definition of the Principal Meridians

Just like blood, energy flows endlessly through our bodies, but it follows channels that are known as Principal Meridians.

There are twelve (12) Principal Meridians and they are named after the organs to which they are connected.

The Principal Meridians are bilateral, which means they always have a left- and a right-hand branch.

There are six yang meridians and six yin meridians.

YANG Meridians	YIN Meridians
Stomach (S)	Spleen (Sp)
Small intestine (SI)	Heart (H)
Large intestine (LI)	Lungs (L)
Gall-Bladder (GB)	Liver (Lv)
Bladder (B)	Kidneys (K)
Triple Heater (TH)	Master of the Heart (MH)

Yang meridians

Yang meridians are sacs or pipes linked to the outside.

The first three:

Food from the outside enters the body via the mouth, travels to the **Stomach**, continues its route into the **Small intestine** and then on to the **Large intestine**, from whence it is expelled through the anus.

The other three meridians connected to the outside:

The Gall-Bladder is a sac that stores the bile produced by the liver before releasing it into the small intestine as required.

The Bladder is a sac that stores the urine produced by the kidneys and releases it outside the body via the urethra.

The Triple Heater is an energy coordination system involved in thermoregulation and the sympathetic nervous system.

Yin meridians

Yin meridians are connected with more delicate organs and are always filled with blood:

The **Spleen** stores and cleans the blood.

The **Heart** pumps blood.

The **Lungs** remove carbon dioxide from the blood and introduce oxygen.

The **Liver** controls and removes toxins from the blood, adjusting its composition.

The **Kidneys** continuously filter the blood to eliminate waste products.

The **Master of the Heart** is the preservation and control system governing the functions of the heart, blood circulation and the pleasure of living.

Energy partnerships

Each yang meridian is coupled to a yin meridian and vice versa.

Thus, the **Stomach meridian** is coupled to the **Spleen meridian**. The Stomach meridian deals with the first part of the digestive process, which takes place in the mouth and in the stomach. The Spleen meridian plays an important role in the second phase of digestion which takes place in the small intestine with the help of the pancreatic juices.

The **Small intestine** and **Heart meridians** are coupled for the following reasons: the small intestine allows the particles resulting from digestion to cross its walls. From this moment, small particles of nutrients are caught up in the blood being pumped by the heart which then distributes them to all our cells.

The **Lungs meridian** is coupled with that of the **Large intestine** because the main function of both these organs is elimination: the lungs eliminate waste gases and the large intestine eliminates solid waste. They also play another role: the lungs absorb oxygen and the large intestine reabsorbs water, mineral salts and certain vitamins.

The **Liver meridian** is coupled with the **Gall-Bladder meridian** because the liver produces bile and the gall-bladder stores it.

The **Kidney meridian** is coupled with the **Bladder meridian** because the kidneys excrete urine which is stored in the bladder.

As for the **Master of the Heart** and the **Triple Heater meridians**, they have to be coupled together because they are responsible for two functions; one yin, which particularly involves the heart and the other, mainly yang, which involves heat and thermoregulation.

The role of the digestive system

Our body is a universe of thousands of millions of cells. We are responsible for the life of these cells, which is why we must feed them. To do this, we possess a digestive system which allows the macroscopic substances we eat to be reduced into tiny particles, corresponding to the absorbency capacities of our cells. The foodstuffs we eat are, therefore, transformed into nutrients adapted to the requirements of our cellular universe.

The law of the five elements

The law of the five elements allows us to understand the reasons behind our tastes, our dislikes, our character. It helps us to build up an energy picture and allows us to better understand our position in relation to the laws of the universe.

Each season has a corresponding dominant element. In spring, it is Wood, in summer it is Fire, in autumn, Metal and in winter it is Water. Earth is sort of interseasonal but its main period of activity is towards the end of summer.

Each element has a corresponding pair of meridians, one or more colours, one or more flavours, a climate, a psychological state, a group of tissues. The tables on the following pages will illustrate this.

The element Earth

The Spleen and Stomach meridians are linked to the element Earth.

The earth feeds us. It produces foodstuffs that keep us alive and which we have to digest with the help of the digestive juices produced by the stomach and the pancreas.

The corresponding colour is yellow. It occupies a central position, just as the stomach, the spleen and the pancreas are in the centre of our body. It corresponds to a damp climate, which is necessary for the earth to be productive, and to a sweet flavour such as that of the carbohydrates that are found in most fruits, cereals and certain vegetables.

Man is in between heaven and earth. He vibrates according to the harmony of the cosmo-telluric waves he receives. For man, the earth represents the universe, of which he is the centre. A well-centred, stable person is said to be well-balanced. This also shows great possibilities for concentration and rapid reflexes in such an individual. Also, the spleen is part of the lymphatic system and someone who possesses a good level of spleen energy will be quick and enterprising, whereas someone who lacks this aspect will be inclined to be lymphatic and liable to 'miss out' on life.

The lymphatic system, flesh and conjunctive tissues are all situated within this element.

The element Metal

The element Metal corresponds to the Lungs and Large Intestine meridians. It is linked with the west, with autumn, with white and with a spicy taste.

The psyche is influenced by autumn which corresponds to an intermediary period between the end of a yang season and the beginning of a yin cycle. It is at this moment that nature puts on its most handsome show, for a relatively short space of time. For a few days, leaves take on magnificent hues, an open invitation to romanticism. Then the leaves fall and nature takes on a melancholy air. By balancing the energy in the Lungs and Large intestine meridians, we can combat such sadness and depression. The element Metal is linked to the skin, the throat and the nose. The skin could be considered as a sort of peripheral lung which breathes, so it is not at all surprising to discover points affecting the skin along the Lung and Large Intestine meridians.

The element Water

The element Water corresponds to winter, the north, the cold and a salty taste. Don't forget that it is in the sea and oceans – which cover 70% of our planet, that salt is found. Apart from the superficial layer of water, the oceans are cold and dark, which is why black is associated with this element.

The Kidney meridian is linked to the element Water, and is also connected with the adrenal glands which produce adrenalin that could be considered as the 'bravery hormone'. Anyone who lacks energy along this meridian will lack courage; fear and the cold will make him 'wet his pants'. A person who has a good energy level along the Kidney meridian will be brave and capable of making the right decisions under any circumstances, whereas someone who is lacking Kidney meridian energy will always be a ditherer. He always takes his time before answering questions and will never come to the point straight away.

This element is linked to the bones, the teeth and the ears. Our bones and teeth need mineral salts and so do our ears, which contain tiny bones that can suffer from osteoporosis and decalcification. It is therefore important, for our bones, that our kidneys remain very selective and do not allow our mineral salts to escape. We also know the importance of cortisone – a hormone produced in the cortex of the adrenal glands – in treating rheumatic pain in bones and joints.

The element Wood

In spring, the dominant colours are blue and green: green in nature and blue in the sky, thanks to the wind which blows the clouds away. People who like blue need the energy given off by this colour, to stimulate their liver. On the other hand, if someone doesn't like wearing green clothes, this could reveal an excess of yang energy in the gall-bladder. From a psychological point of view, the element Wood corresponds to combat. If there is a good balance of energy in the gall-bladder, any individual will be able to fight for his life against germs, laziness, stress and any other elements that attack his well-being. If this energy is lacking, the subject will not be inclined to fight and will lack audacity. However, if there is an excess, in other words, an energy overload, he will easily lose his temper, will tend to be vindictive and may act thoughtlessly, leading to difficult consequences.

In the case of both an excess and a lack of energy, the individual will not be able to face up to various aggressions and will be easily upset. We must therefore treat the Liver and Gall-Bladder meridians in cases of anguish, shyness or impulsiveness.

This element is host to the eyes, the muscles and the nails. In Chinese medicine, it is said that the liver flowers in the eyes. We shall see how to improve sight by using certain points situated on the Liver and Gall-Bladder meridians.

The element Fire

Energy culminates in the element Fire which is represented by four meridians. The Fire Minister by the Master of the Heart and the Triple Heater meridians and the Fire Emperor by the Heart and Small intestine meridians. This element is associated with the colour red, summer, heat and the south. It favours smoky, charred and bitter tastes.

From a psychological point of view, the element Fire represents the reason for living, the love of creation in the universe, or to sum all this up: the Joy of Living, Love, Generosity. When this element is under control, it lends wisdom, serenity and pleasure in a healthy, active and beneficial life. An individual suffering from an excess in the element Fire will be hot-headed and have plenty of colour, will have an easy smile and approach and will always be spontaneous. He will be rather too fond of good food and corrupted pleasures and will be quite likely to 'burn the candle at both ends', resulting in heart and circulation problems.

Individuals lacking in this element will have a dull complexion, be subject to low blood pressure, will lack enthusiasm and optimism and will tend to be listless and fed up with life in general.

The ideal – as in any other field – is to strike the right balance.

This element is associated with the veins and arteries, in other words, the blood circulation. A deficiency connected with the element Fire will cause low blood pressure, whereas an excess will cause high blood pressure.

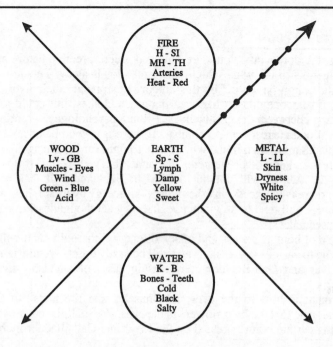

The element Earth, situated in the centre, moves round the seasons, but is dominant towards the end of summer.

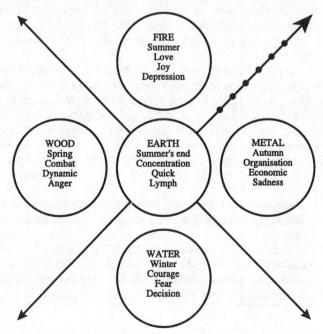

The five elements and the psyche

Element	EARTH	METAL	WATER	WOOD	FIRE
Situation	Central	West	North	East	South
Season	Between seasons Summer's end	Autumn	Winter	Spring	Summer
Climate	Damp	Dry	Cold	Windy	Hot
Colour	Yellow	White	Black	Green/Blue	Red
Flavour	Sweet	Spicy	Salty	Acid	Bitter
Yin meridian	Sp	L	K	Lv	H – MH
Yang meridian	S	LI	B	GB	SI – TH
Functions	Nourishment Digestion	Recovery Evacuation	Filtering Elimination	Production Elim.	Assimilation Delivery Circulation
Organic tissue	Lymph	Skin	Bones and Teeth	Eyes and Muscles	Arteries
Beneficial psychic energy	Balance Concentration	Order Organisation Conservation	Courage Resistance Decision Will-power	Defence Combat Realisation	Satisfaction Intelligence Love Wisdom
Destructive energy	Worries	Sadness	Fear	Anger	Dissatisfaction
Energy overload	Obsession Instability	Imposing ideas	Authoritarian Takes risks Impulsive	Rancour Aggressive	Party-goer Burn candle both ends
Energy deficiency	Lack of balance Lymphatic	Moaner Disorganised	Fear Indecision	Worrier	Depression Fed up with life

Table of the five elements and their relationships

Boosting and dispersion

We have three possibilities:
1. To boost or disperse the whole body;
2. To boost or disperse just one area or a specific function;
3. To boost or disperse a meridian.

To do this, we can use:
1. Specific points that influence the whole body;
2. Points that influence just one area or a specific function;
3. Control points on the meridian which treat this meridian.

To boost the whole body, we use 'general influence' points which must be boosted, such as the *antitiredness points*, as follows:

6Sp, 36S, 6CV, 4GV, 12CV and 38B.

To disperse the whole body, for example in the case of *an excess of yang energy* in an overexcited subject, we disperse points which have a general relaxing influence, as follows:

6MH, 3Lv, 4LI, 40GB and 17CV.

To boost a meridian, we must stimulate the meridian's booster point or its source.

To disperse a meridian, we must stimulate the meridian's dispersion point or its source.

Note: Each meridian's booster and dispersion points change with the seasons. Details concerning this will be given as we move on to study the Principal Meridians.

The most important points on the Principal Meridians

The following five points are always found on each Principal Meridian and are located at the end of the members, either between the toes and knee or between the fingers and elbow.

The Booster point
This increases the proportion of yang energy in the corresponding meridian.

The Dispersion point
This reduces the proportion of yang energy in the corresponding meridian.

The Source
This can boost or disperse the corresponding meridian, as required.

The Lo point
This point promotes harmony within the yin-yang partnership and allows an excess of energy in a given meridian to be passed over to its partner meridian, which is lacking in energy.

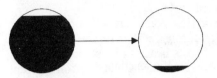

Cross-section of 2 Principal Meridians showing imbalance

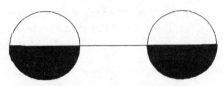

Cross-section of 2 Principal Meridians showing balance

The Ting point
The Ting point is located at the base of the nail, as shown opposite. This is either the first or the last point on the Principal meridian. All meridians begin or end at the base of a nail, except the Kidney Principal meridian, which starts on the sole of the foot.

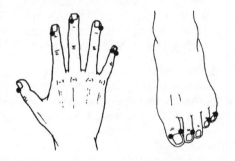

Note: The number of points varies from one meridian to another. For example, the Master of the Heart PM has 9, whereas the Bladder PM has 67. But all meridians have a point for boosting them, another for dispersing them, a Source which can complete the action of the Booster or the Dispersion point and a Lo point which balances the pair. All these points are at the extremities of members, below the knee or the elbow, along with the Key points which influence the Extraordinary Vessels. The other points influence a function or a specific area of the body.

Special points

The Key point
There are 8 Key points on each side of the body, four on the foot and four on the hand. These points are extremely important since they open up Extraordinary Vessels and regulate several Principal Meridians in one go and treat several disorders all at once.

The Mo point
This point is situated on the trunk. It has a direct influence on the corresponding organ to which it is connected. As a rule, it is stimulated along with the corresponding Lu point.

The Lu point
This point is found on the back, on the Bladder PM, on either side of the muscles along the spine. It is a reflex point acting directly on the organ it represents.

Important information on points that boost and disperse

We must not confuse boosting or dispersing a meridian and boosting or dispersing a point.

Only the Source, Booster or Dispersion points can boost or disperse a meridian. All other points on the meridian can boost or disperse a function or the specific area to which they are connected.

In addition, only the Booster and Dispersion points are influenced by the seasons and therefore can boost the meridian during a certain season and disperse it during another. For example, point 9L boosts better in its season, which is autumn, but as it is a Source point, it can also boost during other seasons, except in summer when it disperses. In other words, if we want to disperse the meridian in summer, we use point 9L and if we want to boost it, we stimulate point 11L which is a booster during this season.

It is interesting to note that all Booster and Dispersion points are always at the extremities of members, below the elbow or the knee. There are no meridian Booster or Dispersion points on the trunk. However, points on the trunk can be boosted or dispersed simply for themselves, such as point 2L which acts on its surrounding area, that is to say, below the clavicle or on the lungs.

For the ladies

Never stimulate points during your period. Point 60B is the only one that can be touched during these few days (for dispersion). It relieves pain.

60B: Situated just behind the lateral malleolus.

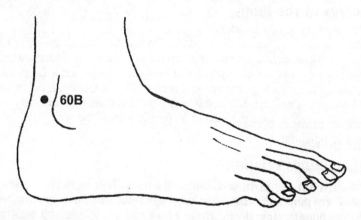

You are also advised to avoid certain points during pregnancy. These are listed under **Precautions**.

CHAPTER 3

Principal Meridians

Energy physiology and the most important points

Lung PM

Polarity:	Yin
Partner meridian:	Large intestine
PM Element:	Metal
Season:	Autumn
Colour:	White
Situation:	West
Organic tissue:	Skin
Organic function:	Recovering oxygen and evacuating waste gases
Psychic energy:	Romanticism, sadness
Energy peak:	Between 3 am and 5 am

Physiology of the lungs

The role of the lungs is to allow oxygen to be absorbed by the blood and carbon dioxide to be evacuated.

Oxygen is absolutely vital for chemical reactions that take place within body cells and which maintain life. But these reactions produce carbon dioxide which has to be eliminated as quickly as possible.

This two-way traffic takes place in the alveoli in the lungs, thanks to a difference in pressure between the outside and the inside and a difference in electro-ionic potential.

The heart/lungs relationship

Our heartbeat is influenced by our respiratory rhythm and vice versa. It is perfectly possible to slow down a heartbeat that has been accelerated due to exercise, by taking several deep, controlled breaths. Using this technique, yogis can control their bodily functions. This link between the heart and the lungs explains why certain points on the Lung PM have an influence on the arteries and the blood pressure, for example point 9L.

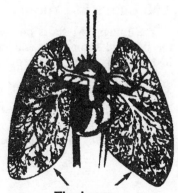

The lungs

The physiology of Lungs PM energy

The Lungs/Large intestine couple belongs to the Metal element, situated in autumn, a romantically inclined season thanks to its atmosphere: the wonderful hues of nature, a gentle climate, time for harvesting and preserving the fruits of nature. It is time to start organising things for winter which is fast approaching. At the end of autumn, the leaves fall, the days grow shorter and the cold settles around us. Sadness invades us, too: "There are mounds and mounds of dead leaves, of memories and sorrow." This is how romanticism drifts into melancholy.

And it is easy to see a note of pessimism in the behaviour of people whose Lungs and Large intestine Principal Meridians are lacking energy. This is why it is a good idea to boost these meridians, to stop such people complaining incessantly.

In view of the above, you will understand why it is necessary to balance this electro-ionic potential by stimulating the harmonisation points. Point 9L is an excellent one to stimulate because it is both a Booster point in autumn, the most delicate time of year, and a Source point for the rest of the year, which confers upon it the ability to improve the respiratory function, not only in the lungs, but also – and especially – in our body cells. This explains its beneficial action on the whole of our body, which comprises thousands of millions of living cells.

Point 9L influences:

1. Nervousness and sleep; we must not forget that our nerve cells require 5 times more oxygen than other cell types.
2. The arteries, the blood quality and blood pressure. (Blood which is richer in oxygen and contains less carbon dioxide is more fluid and can avoid clots. It flows more easily through our blood vessels and makes us feel more energetic.)
3. Sadness, pessimism and melancholy. (We have already seen the Law of the 5 elements, which shows that energy deficiencies in the Lung PM lead to feelings of sadness. Now we understand why it is so beneficial to boost point 9L in subjects who feel sad and sorry for themselves. It is also a good idea to stimulate the Joy of Living point, 3H, which we shall examine along with the Heart PM.

The Lungs PM route

The Lungs PM starts on the thorax, between the first and second ribs and ends on the thumb, level with the outer corner of the nail.

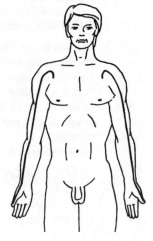

Pain along the course of the Lungs PM

Pain in the thumb, on the thumb side of the wrist, in the forearm, in the centre of the front of the elbow, level with the biceps or on the front of the shoulder.

What to do if you feel pain along the course of the Lungs PM

Boost the Ting point on both sides	11L+
Boost the Booster point on the same side as the pain	9L+
Disperse the points surrounding the pain	–
Boost the Meeting point on both sides	22GB+

Symptoms of an energy excess in the Lungs PM

Coughing, sneezing, dry and tickly throat, dry nose, abnormally compliant behaviour.

How to disperse the Lungs PM in the event of such excess

In spring:	10L-	In autumn:	5L-
In summer:	9L-	In winter:	1L-
End of summer:	8L-		

Symptoms of an energy deficiency in the Lungs PM

Frequent sore throats, pale complexion, low blood pressure, tired voice.

How to boost the Lungs PM in the case of deficiency

In spring:	5L+	In autumn:	9L+
In summer:	11L+	In winter:	8L+
End of summer:	10L+		

The most important points on the Lungs PM

1L: *Mo point*
This is located on the upper edge of the second rib, beneath point 2L from which it is separated by the first rib. Acts directly on the lungs.
In the case of a cold, avoids catching influenza (+).
Cough with inflammation of the lungs (-).

2L: Located in the lower hollow of the clavicle, which is accentuated by bringing the shoulder forward. Acts directly on the lungs.
In the case of a cold, avoids catching influenza (+).
Cough with inflammation of the lungs (-).

5L: Located in the middle of the crease of the elbow, touching the tendon of the biceps. This point disperses the Lungs meridian during its season – autumn – but boosts it in spring. In all seasons, it can treat the following disorders:
Sneezing (-).
Painful elbows (-).

7L: *An important Key point*
Lo point
This is located in the radial groove, where you can feel the pulse, 3 fingerbreadths

above the wrist crease, that is to say, above the radial styloid.
To stop a bout of asthma in its tracks (-).
To stop a cough in its tracks (-).
To soothe a burn or sunburn (-).

8L: Located in the radial groove, level with the radial styloid. This point boosts the Lungs meridian in winter and disperses it at the end of summer. In all seasons, it can treat the following disorders:
Pain in the hand, the wrist or the thumb (-).
Laryngitis (-).
Dry nose (-).

9L: *Source point*
Starter point for sleep, located in the radial groove, on the wrist crease, in other words before the radial styloid. This point boosts the Lungs meridian during its season – autumn – but disperses it in summer. In all seasons, it can treat the following disorders:
Has a beneficial influence on the arteries. Gives you extra energy in the case of low blood pressure (+).
Gives you extra energy in the case of sadness (+), when combined with 36S (+), 6Sp (+) and 3H (-).

10L: Located right in the centre of the first metacarpal, on the thenar eminence, level with the inside of the origin of the thumb muscle. This point boosts the Lungs meridian at the end of the summer and disperses it in spring. In all seasons, it can treat the following disorders:
Painful thumb (-).
Voice loss due to a sore throat (-).
Alcoholic intoxication (-).

11L: *Ting point*
Located at the corner of the thumbnail. This point boosts the Lungs meridian in summer and disperses it in winter. In all seasons, it can treat the following disorders:
Sore throat (+). Very effective in children.

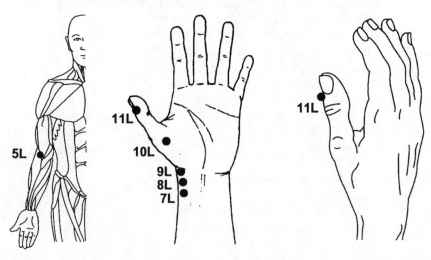

Large intestine PM

Polarity:	Yang
Partner meridian:	Lungs PM
Element:	Metal
Season:	Autumn
Colour:	White
Situation:	West
Organic tissue:	Skin
Organic function:	Recovering and evacuating solid waste
Psychic energy:	Romanticism, sadness
Optimum energy:	Between 5 am and 7 am

Physiology of the Large intestine

Substances that are not absorbed during previous digestion phases end up in the large intestine, which is only 1.5 metres long but whose diameter is three times greater than that of the small intestine. Defaecation is not the only function performed by the large intestine; important operations take place here such as the production of certain vitamins, for example, vitamin K and vitamin B. Some of the water and mineral salts contained in waste are reabsorbed from the large intestine. Food which has not been digested is pushed towards the outside. This is the final phase of the digestive process.

The Physiology of Large intestine PM energy

We have seen that the Large intestine PM is coupled with the Lungs PM; it belongs to the Metal element, is situated in autumn, the harvest season (recovery, bringing in), for preservation (organisation, planning ahead), and fertilisers (recovering what has been eliminated, ie, exit = entrance). Autumn implies a certain amount of organisation, accounting for everything that has been taken into and left the body. Thus, the large intestine is responsible for recovering water from digested matter, along with mineral salts and vitamins, while it eliminates waste which can be used as fertiliser to regenerate organic life in the Earth.

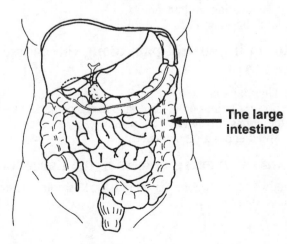

The large intestine

Individuals suffering from a lack of large intestine energy can have difficulty in being organised and keeping their ideas – and life in general – in order.

However, individuals who suffer from excess energy are quite likely to be sticklers for organisation, be excessively critical and want to impose their ideas on everyone.

An energy deficiency in the large intestine can therefore cause constipation due to the lack of tonus in its muscles, or diarrhoea, or even problems with organisation or energy savings.

Point 11LI is therefore the ideal point to stimulate, since it is the large intestine's Booster point in autumn and can help cure constipation due to sluggish digestion, straightforward diarrhoea, skin disorders such as dry skin, acne or a rash, as well as righting people's lack of organisation or their poor management of their own energy potential. Outside autumn, other points should be stimulated: point 1LI in winter, 2LI in spring and 4LI in summer.

Route taken by the Large intestine PM

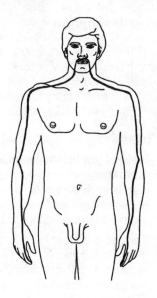

The Large intestine PM starts at the corner of the nail of the forefinger, alongside the thumb, runs up the outer side of the forearm, the upper arm and the neck to end at the nose.

Pain along the course of the Large intestine PM

You should not be at all surprised to discover that pain that is felt in the forefinger, the wrist, the elbow (tennis elbow), the shoulder, the throat, the teeth – or a blocked nose – is connected with a problem in the large intestine and that such pain can be treated by stimulating certain points along the large intestine PM.

What to do if you feel pain along the course of the Large intestine PM

Boost the Ting point on both sides:	1LI +
Boost the Booster point on the same side as the pain:	11LI +
Disperse the points surrounding the pain:	–
Boost the Meeting point on both sides:	13GB +

Symptoms of an energy excess in the Large intestine PM

Spasmodic constipation, hard and dark stools, acute diarrhoea with inflammation, colitis.

How to disperse the Large intestine PM in the case of an excess

In spring:	5LI-	In autumn:	2LI-
In summer:	11LI-	In winter:	3LI-
End of summer:	1LI-		

Symptoms of an energy deficiency in the Large intestine PM

Constipation due to sluggish digestion, a lazy large intestine, straightforward diarrhoea.

How to boost the Large intestine PM in the case of deficiency

In spring:	2LI+	In autumn:	11LI+
In summer:	3LI+	In winter:	1LI+
End of summer:	5LI+		

The most important points on the Large intestine PM

1LI: *Ting point*
Located at the corner of the thumb side of the forefinger nail.
This point boosts the Large intestine meridian in winter and disperses it at the end of the summer. In all seasons, it can treat the following disorders:
Sore throat (+).
Toothache (+).
Acne (+).

2LI: Located just before the metacarpal/phalanx joint, on the inner side of the forefinger.
This point disperses the Large intestine meridian during its season – autumn – and boosts it in spring. In all seasons, it can treat the following disorder:
Painful forefinger (-).

3LI: Located just after the metacarpal/phalanx joint, on the inner edge.
This point disperses the Large Intestine meridian in spring and boosts it in summer. In all seasons, it can treat the following disorders:
Rumbling stomach (+).
Flatulence (+).

4LI: Located in the angle formed by the first two metacarpals, touching the base of the second metacarpal, it can treat the following disorders:
Sluggish constipation (+).
Straightforward diarrhoea (+).
Fainting (+).
Constipation due to spasms (small, dry, 'strangled' stools) (-).
Diarrhoea due to inflammation of the colon (-).
Headaches (-).
Precaution: Do not stimulate during pregnancy.

5LI: Located in the hollow above the thumb. This point disperses the Large intestine meridian in spring. In all seasons, it can treat the following disorders:
Painful thumb (-).
Dry skin (-).

11LI: Located at the outer limit of the elbow crease. This point boosts the Large intestine meridian during its season – autumn – and disperses it in summer. In all seasons, it can treat the following disorders:
Sluggish constipation (+).
Dry skin (+).
Eczema (+).
Acne (+).

20LI: Located in the hollow just below the outer edge of the nostril.
Used to stimulate the lip muscles (+).
To unblock a stuffy nose (-).

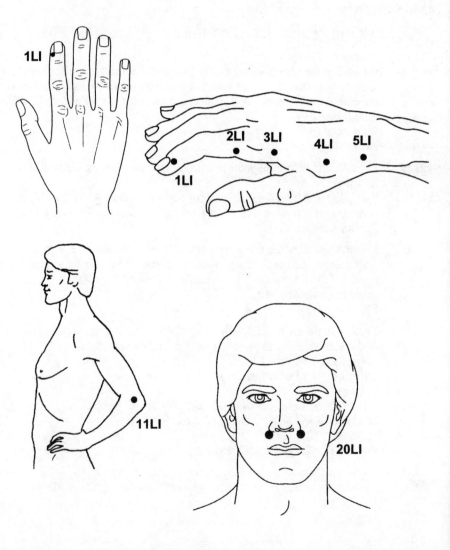

The Stomach PM

Polarity:	Yang
Partner meridian:	Spleen
PM Element:	Earth
Season:	End of summer
Colour:	Yellow
Situation:	Central
Organic tissue:	Lymph
Organic function:	Nourishment and digestion
Psychic energy:	Balance, stability, digestion of food and worries
Energy peak:	Between 7 am and 9 am

Physiology of the Stomach

The purpose of digestion is to break down the foodstuffs, provided by the Earth, into the microscopic particles required for feeding our cells.

In fact, there are two phases to the digestive process. The first involves the Stomach PM and consists of choosing – with the help of our senses of sight and smell – the food we wish to eat, then it will be chewed, mixed with saliva, swallowed and sent down to the stomach, where the bolus will be attacked by hydrochloric acid and pepsin, two substances elaborated by the stomach cells and controlled by the the hormone gastrin, which regulates the production of gastric juices as required.

The stomach wall is made up of smooth muscle tissue, which allows this organ to grind food in order to impregnate it thoroughly with gastric juices before expelling it into the small intestine once this first digestive phase is completed.

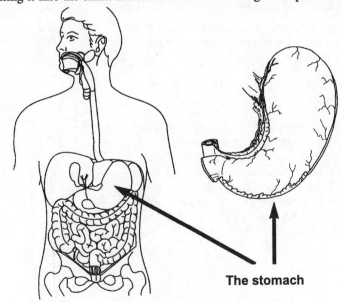

The stomach

The physiology of Stomach PM energy

We have seen that the first digestive phase corresponds to the Stomach PM. Observe its course on the diagram below. You will see that it begins beneath the eyes, runs down each side of the nose, then to the salivary glands. This meridian exactly follows the start of the digestive process, in other words, before eating, we look at our plate, we smell it, then salivate while we chew our food before swallowing it. The seventh point on this meridian acts on the muscle used for chewing. By dispersing this point, we can get rid of cramp in our jaws (which can be due to an excess of yang energy), whereas if we boost it, we brighten up our face. Level with the throat, we find points 9S and 10S which treat the throat and the action of swallowing. And it is no coincidence to find there is a point on the nipple, belonging to the Stomach PM, which allows a newborn baby to fill up its stomach by practising 'suckling presso-puncture' as soon as it is born (17S). The Stomach PM continues down across the stomach, the thighs, and the outside of the legs to the centre of the sole of the foot – where our whole body is balanced. We must not forget that the stomach is in charge of controlling our energy balance, among other things, both in a literal and a figurative sense (see the Law of the 5 elements). Obviously, this point is toned up by walking, and walking helps digestion after a meal, it also sharpens our appetite before a meal and it helps us maintain our inner balance.

All along this meridian, we find points with a physiological influence on the first phase of digestion, the teeth, the jaw muscles, the stomach, but also our physical and psychic balance. This is why, if we want to be on top form, it is vital to maintain the correct energy balance along our Stomach PM, which will allow us to digest properly: both foodstuffs and what we learn.

The Stomach PM route

The Stomach meridian starts below the eye and ends at the corner of the nail of the second toe, alongside the third toe.

Pain along the course of the Stomach PM

It is not at all surprising to discover that facial neuralgia can be connected with the Stomach PM, as can certain cases of toothache, sore throats, painful breasts, stomach-ache, soreness in the outer thighs or the knees, along the outside of the tibia, the foot or the second or third toes. Indeed, these two toes are often deformed in subjects suffering from stomach troubles.

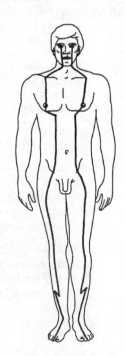

What to do if you feel pain along the course of the Stomach PM

Boost the Ting point on both sides	45S+
Boost the Booster point on the same side as the pain	41S+
Disperse the points surrounding the pain	–
Boost the Meeting point on both sides	2S+

Symptoms of an energy excess in the Stomach PM

Stomach cramps and heartburn, eating too fast, acid stomach, gastritis, impatience, with a tendency to precipitate matters.

How to disperse the Stomach PM in the event of such excess

In spring:	41S-	In autumn:	44S-
In summer:	36S-	In winter:	43S-
End of summer:	45S-		

Symptoms of an energy deficiency in the Stomach PM

Slow digestion, lazy stomach, a tendency to worry about nothing, anorexia, headaches in which the pain is concentrated above the eyebrows.

How to boost the Stomach PM in the case of deficiency

In spring:	44S+	In autumn:	36S+
In summer:	43S+	In winter:	45S+
End of summer:	41S+		

The most important points on the Stomach PM

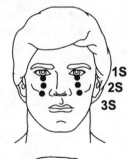

1S: This is located right in the centre of the hollow beneath the eye.
Blinking (-).
Blurred sight (-).

2S: Located in the hollow just underneath point 1S.
To reduce swollen eyelids (-).

3S: Located in the hollow 2 fingerbreadths to either side of the nostrils.
Maxillary sinusitis (-).
Red eyes in short-sighted subjects (-).
Malfunctions in the sense of smell (+).

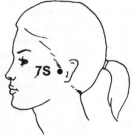

7S: Located in front of the ear, in the hollow formed when the mouth is opened.
To fortify the facial muscles (+).
To relax contraction of the jaw muscles (-).
To treat acne (-).
Runny saliva (+).

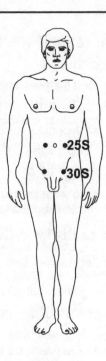

25S: *Mo point of the Large intestine*
Located 3 fingerbreadths to either side of the navel.
Flatulence (+).
Sluggish constipation (+).
Diarrhoea (+).
Constipation with spasms (-).
Colitis (-).

30S: *Nutritional Master point*
Energy stores
Located above the pubis, 3 fingerbreadths from the median line.
Distribution of energy from the 3 centres to the 12 PMs (-).
Sterility (+).
Impotence (+).
Menstruation problems (-).
Painful testicles (-).
Insufficient erection (+).
To assist birth and stimulate the expulsion of the placenta (-).

32S: *Master point governing veins*
Located in the centre of the front of the outer side of the thigh.
Tired legs (-).
Varicose veins (-).
To activate blood circulation in the legs, and to warm them up (-).
Pins and needles in the legs (-).

36S: Located 4 fingerbreadths below the knee, between the two muscles.
THE MOST IMPORTANT POINT OF ALL.
Boosts the Stomach PM in autumn and disperses it in winter. In all seasons, it can treat the following disorders:

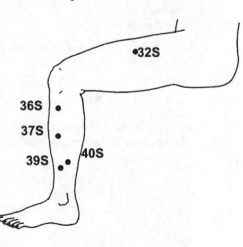

To boost the whole body and raise the blood pressure (+, in the morning, except in summer)
To stimulate digestion (+).
To give yourself more energy (+), (preferably in the morning).
To recover balance (+).
To soothe seasickness (+).
To soothe nervousness (-).
To soothe heartburn and stomach cramps (-), combined with 45S (-) and 12CV (-).

37S: Located just above the centre of the lower leg, 4 fingerbreadths below point 36S.
Diarrhoea (+).

39S: Located 7 fingerbreadths above the lateral malleolus.
Dry skin (+).
Dry hair (+).
Corns (+).
Verrucas on the sole of the foot (+).
Pain in the knees when descending stairs (-).
Phantom members, if the stump is painful (+, on the opposite side).

40S: *Lo point*
Located almost halfway up the lower leg, 2 fingerbreadths from the tibial ridge, slightly above and outside point 39S, between the muscles, in front of the fibula.
Overexcitement (-).
Dizziness (+).
Facial neuralgia (+, on the opposite side)
Congested face and nose (+).
Acute chest pain (+).
Precaution: Do not stimulate this point after the 6th month of pregnancy.

41S: *Booster point, except in spring*
Located right in the centre of the front of the ankle, in the hollow between the tendons. Stimulated during walking. Helps digestion and sharpens the appetite, which is why it is good to take a walk before a meal.
This point boosts the Stomach meridian during its season – the end of summer – and disperses it in spring. **Note:** The booster action of point 41S is particularly obvious in between seasons, towards the end of summer, ie, between 15th August and 5th September, and during damp periods. In all seasons, it can treat the following disorders:
To help balance (+).
To fight anorexia (+).
Ophthalmic migraine (+).

42S: *Source point*
Located on the upper side of the foot, 3 fingerbreadths below point 41S.
Subjects who feel the cold (+).
Tooth problems (+).

43S: Located on the upper side of the foot, between the second and third metatarsals.
This point boosts the Stomach meridian in summer and disperses it in winter. In all seasons, it can treat the following disorders:
Painful feet (-).
Shivering (-).
Malaria (-).
Nocturnal sweating (-).

44S: Located between the second and third toes. Specifically linked with nightmares.
This point boosts the Stomach meridian in spring and disperses it in autumn. In all seasons, it can treat the following disorders:
Nightmares (-).
Stuttering (-), combined with points 6MH (-) and 5H (+).

45S: *Ting point*
Dispersion point
Located at the corner of the nail of the second toe, alongside the third toe. This point disperses the Stomach meridian during its season – the end of summer – and boosts it in winter.
Note: The dispersing action of point 45S is particularly obvious in between seasons, especially towards the end of summer, ie, between 15th August and 5th September, and during damp periods. In all seasons, it can treat the following disorders:
To suppress excessive appetite (-), combined with point 36S (-).
To soothe heartburn (-), combined with point 36S.
Precaution: Do not stimulate this point during the sixth month of pregnancy.

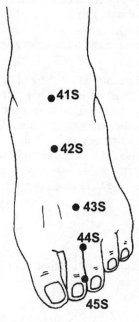

The Spleen PM

Polarity:	Yin
Partner meridian:	Stomach
PM Element:	Earth
Season:	End of summer
Colour:	Yellow
Situation:	Central
Organic tissue:	Lymph
Organic function:	Nourishment and digestion
Psychic energy:	Concentration, digestion of food and worries, synoptic capacity
Energy peak:	Between 9 am and 11 am

Physiology of the Spleen and the Pancreas

This meridian is connected with energy in the spleen and the pancreas. The right-hand meridian is apparently more closely connected to the pancreas and the left-hand one more closely linked with the spleen.

What is the spleen? It is an organ filled with blood, which is part of the lymph system. The spleen produces blood (white blood cells) as required. It stores and distributes blood under certain circumstances. It clears the blood of dead or defective red blood cells and waste. This gland plays an important role in the blood circulation system, which is why the master point of the blood, point 6Sp, is found on this meridian. This point acts mainly on blood clotting, circulation and especially menstruation, which it can regulate. The spleen also elaborates antibodies to neutralise dangerous elements circulating in the lymph and the blood.

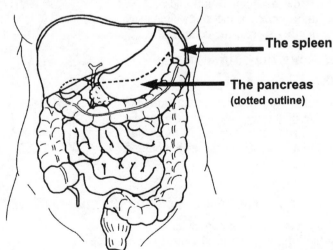

The spleen

The pancreas
(dotted outline)

What is the pancreas?

It is a large, long gland, measuring about 15 cm long. Like the spleen, it is found in the centre of the body, close to the stomach. It is an endocrine gland (secreting directly into the blood) and is responsible for the production of insulin and glucagon which regulate the amount of glucose in the blood, stocking any excess in the liver when it needs to be reduced. Glucagon stimulates the restitution of glucose back into the blood when required. But the pancreas is also an exocrine gland, in other words it secretes through ducts, and plays an important role in the process of digestion, during the intestinal phase. The pancreas can secrete between 1.5 and 2.5 litres of pancreatic juice into the small intestine, thus completing the digestive process started in the stomach. The Spleen meridian is therefore also involved in digestion.

The physiology of Spleen PM energy

We have seen that the spleen is part of the lymph system and that it is coupled with the Stomach PM in the Earth element; it is centrally situated, which helps the speed of any movement in any direction. So it is not at all surprising to find that subjects suffering from a spleen energy deficiency are lymphatic and likely to miss out on important opportunities. However, individuals who have an excess of spleen energy will often 'go overboard', try too hard, be permanently preoccupied and not be able to sit still.

Hence the advantage of being well-balanced, which means one can concentrate, have fast and effective reflexes, and be perfectly capable of reasoning normally.

The route taken by the Spleen PM

The Spleen meridian starts at the inner corner of the big toenail and ends on the side of the thorax, in the sixth intercostal space, in other words, the centre.

Pain along the course of the Spleen PM

Painful big toes, bunions, pain along the inner side of the leg, the rear edge of the tibia, the inside of the knee, the inner side of the thigh, the crotch, the abdomen and the thorax.

What to do if you feel pain along the course of the Spleen PM

Boost the Ting point on both sides	1Sp+
Boost the Booster point on the same side as the pain	2Sp+
Disperse the points surrounding the pain	−
Boost the Meeting point on both sides	3CV+

Symptoms of an energy excess in the Spleen PM

Hot flushes, insufficient menstruation, tendency to obsessive behaviour.

How to disperse the Spleen PM in the event of such excess

In spring:	2Sp-	In autumn:	9Sp-
In summer:	3Sp-	In winter:	1Sp-
End of summer:	5Sp-		

Symptoms of an energy deficiency in the Spleen PM

Tiredness in the morning, difficulty in concentrating, low blood sugar level, excessive bleeding during menstruation or long periods, lymph.

How to boost the Spleen PM in the case of deficiency

In spring:	9Sp+	In autumn:	3Sp+
In summer:	1Sp+	In winter:	5Sp+
End of summer:	2Sp+		

The most important points on the Spleen PM

1Sp: *Ting point*
Located at the inner corner of the big toenail.
This point disperses the Spleen meridian in winter and boosts it in summer. In all seasons, it can treat the following disorders:
To activate lymph circulation (+).
To help regulate menstruation (+).
To reduce haemorrhoids (+), combined with points 57B, 1GV and 28B (-).

2Sp: Located on the inner edge of the foot, just in front of the big toe joint.
This point boosts the Spleen meridian in its season – the end of summer – and disperses it in spring.
Note: The booster action of point 2Sp is particularly obvious in between seasons, especially towards the end of summer, ie, between 15th August and 5th September, and during damp periods. In all seasons, it can treat the following disorders:
An aid to concentration, and it can help youngsters to solve their Maths problems (+, but not in spring)
To activate growth (+).
To fight against morning tiredness (+).
Abscesses (+).
Precaution: Do not stimulate this point during the first month of pregnancy.

3Sp: *Source point*
Located behind the metatarsal/phalanx joint.
This point boosts the Spleen meridian in autumn and disperses it in summer.
In all seasons, it can treat the following disorders:
Painful big toe (-).
Cramp (-).
Painful joints caused by damp (-).

41

4Sp: *Key point of the Tchrong Mo Extraordinary vessel*
Specific to hormone disorders, particularly concerning the ovaries and the thyroid gland.
Located in the centre of the inner side of the foot, on the border between the dorsal skin and the sole of the foot.
Loss of menstruation (-).
Insufficient menstruation (-).
Diarrhoea (+).
Gastric wind with a feeling of sleepiness after meals (-).
Painful testicles (-).
Heart palpitations (-), combined with point 6MH (-).

5Sp: *Master point governing Veins*
Located in front of the medial malleolus, inside the tendon attaching the leg muscle, in the hollow that forms when the foot is turned inwards.
This point disperses the Spleen meridian in its season – the end of summer – and boosts it in winter.
Note: The dispersing action of point 5Sp is particularly obvious in between seasons, especially towards the end of summer, ie, between August 15th and September 5th, and during damp periods. In all seasons, it can treat the following disorders:
Tired legs (-).
Varicose veins (-).
Sluggish circulation (-).
Haemorrhoids (-).
Painful joints without swelling (-).
If joints are swollen, stimulate point 5TH
Painful big toe (-).
Obsession (-).

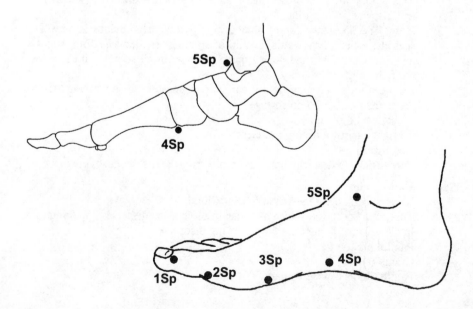

6Sp: *Master point controlling the blood*
Located on the inner side of the leg, 4 fingerbreadths above the medial malleolus, in a hollow behind the tibia.
Improves general and sexual condition (+).
Helps wounds heal (+).
Reduces excessive menstruation (+).
Increases insufficient menstruation (-).
Soothes tired legs (-).
Helps improve circulation (-).

9Sp: *Master point governing Smooth muscle tissue and the Genital organs*
Located on the inner side of the knee, touching the joint.
This point boosts the Spleen meridian in spring and disperses it in autumn.
In all seasons, it can treat the following disorders:
To calm spasms (-).
To soothe abdominal pain, in particular in the uterus (-).
Precaution: Do not stimulate this point after the fifth month of pregnancy.

10Sp: *Master point governing the Blood*
Located on the upper side of the thigh, slightly towards the inside, in a hollow 4 fingerbreadths above the knee.
Combined with point 6Sp, it acts on menstruation and PMT.
Excessive bleeding and blood clots during menstruation (+).
Loss of, or insufficient menstruation (-).
To lower the body temperature in the case of fever (-).

21Sp: *Exit point for this meridian*, which follows on from the Heart PM.
Located on the side of the thorax, in the sixth intercostal space, ie, in the centre.
Disperse this point if it is painful (-).
Dyspnoea (-).
Tension is released at this point, and blood circulation is made easier.
Heart pain (-).

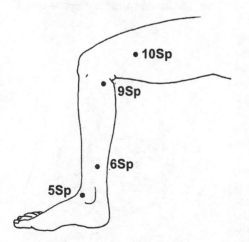

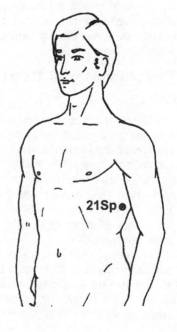

The Heart Principal Meridian

Polarity:	Yin
Partner meridian:	Small intestine PM
Element:	Fire
Season:	Summer
Colour:	Red
Situation:	South
Organic tissue:	Arteries
Organic function:	Blood circulation
Psychic energy:	Love, joy, generosity, neurasthenia
Energy peak:	Between 11 am and 1 pm

Physiology of the Heart

The heart pumps blood through the circulation system and particularly through the arteries. The fundamental function of arterial circulation is to transport oxygen from the lungs and particles of foodstuffs from the small intestine.

You will remember that the function performed by the cells of the small intestine is assimilation, in other words, allowing minute particles of foodstuffs to cross its walls into the arteries, which then distribute these nutritional elements to all our body cells, letting them cross their walls all along the length of these vessels which keep branching out until they reach the microcirculation system of capillaries. If, for any reason whatsoever, this microcirculation is deficient in the brain, such serious problems as hemiplegia can result.

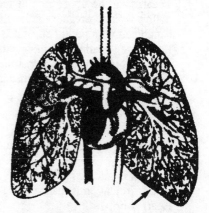

The cardio-respiratory system

The physiology of Heart PM energy

This meridian is involved not only with the cardio-circulatory functions but it is also synonymous with love and generosity. Once again, thanks to this extraordinary science, we can understand the meaning and the link between popular beliefs and the physiology of the energy of the organ under consideration.

In Chinese writings, dating back thousands of years, the heart, which is situated in Fire according to the Law of the 5 elements, represented the Emperor. In those days, the Emperor

Front view of the heart

44

was considered to be God's representative on Earth, with the power of giving life or taking it away. The heart also gives or removes life. Life and death are ascertained by listening to the heart beating. What could be more extraordinary than life? We must worship it and respect it. The love of life is also the love of creation, of creators and creatures. It is the joy of living, laughing, speaking...

You will now understand why we can find points on this meridian to comfort subjects that are depressed: point 3H is known as the 'joy of living' point; point 7H can calm both mental agitation and high blood pressure; point 8H is known as the generosity point and is situated in the hollow of the hand (ready to be held out to those in need). As for point 9H, in the little finger, this allows us to recover the power of speech in the event of it being lost because of an emotional shock.

The route taken by the Heart PM

The Heart PM starts in the armpit and ends at the corner of the little fingernail, alongside the fourth finger.

Pain along the course of the Heart PM

Pain or swelling in the armpit, along the inner side of the front of the arm, the elbow, the inner side of the front of the forearm, the cubital edge of the wrist, the palm of the hand (hypothenar eminence) or the little finger.

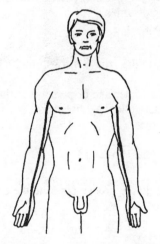
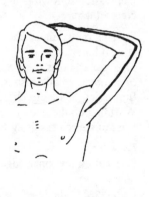

What to do if you feel pain along the course of the Heart PM

Boost the Ting point on both sides	9H+
Boost the Booster point on the same side as the pain	7H+
	except in summer
Disperse the points surrounding the pain	–
Boost the Meeting point on both sides	22GB+

Symptoms of an energy excess in the Heart PM

High blood pressure (especially the diastolic value), red and congested face, moodiness.

How to disperse the Heart PM

In spring:	8H-	In autumn:	3H-
In summer:	7H-	In winter:	9H-
End of summer:	4H-		

Symptoms of an energy deficiency in the Heart PM

Low blood pressure, pallor, depression, breathlessness at the slightest effort.

How to boost the Heart PM

In spring:	3H+	In autumn:	7H+
In summer:	9H+	In winter:	4H+
End of summer:	8H+		

The most important points on the Heart PM

3H: *The 'Joy of living' point*
Located on the crease formed when the elbow is bent, level with the joint. This point boosts the Heart meridian in spring and disperses it in autumn. In all seasons, it can treat the following disorders:
Depression following an emotional shock (-).
Neurasthenia (-).

4H: Located on the inner edge of the wrist, in the groove just before the small styloid bone.
This point boosts the Heart meridian in winter and disperses it at the end of summer. In all seasons, it can treat the following disorders:
Improving blood circulation in the arteries (+).
Warming up the body (+).
Loss of speech resulting from an emotional shock (+).

5H: *Lo point*
Located on the inner edge of the wrist, in the groove opposite the styloid bone.
Pain close to the heart (+).
Palpitations (+).
Low blood pressure (+).
Nerves (+).

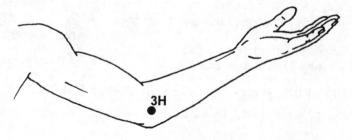

Anguish (+).
Shyness (+).
Anxiety (+).

7H: *Source point*
Located on the wrist crease, just outside the pisiform (small pea-shaped bone).
This point disperses the Heart meridian in its season – summer – and boosts it in autumn. In all seasons except autumn, it can treat the following disorders:
High blood pressure (particularly the diastolic value) (-).
Tachycardia (-).
Hysteria (-).
Nervousness (-).
Congested face (-).
Insomnia due to nervousness (-).

8H: *The Heart's seasonal point in summer*
Located on the palm of the hand, on the heart line, between the fourth and fifth metacarpals. Favours generosity – a 'heart of gold'.
This point boosts the Heart meridian at the end of summer and disperses it in spring.
Neurasthenia (+, in summer)
Lassitude (+, in summer)
High blood pressure (-, in spring)

9H: *Ting point*
Located at the corner of the little fingernail, alongside the fourth finger.
This point boosts the Heart meridian in its season – summer – and disperses it in winter. In all seasons, it can treat the following disorders:
To stimulate the heart (+).
To increase blood pressure (+).
To help fight depression (+).
To relieve pain due to angina (+).
To bring round subjects who have fainted (+).
To recover speech in the case of shock (-).

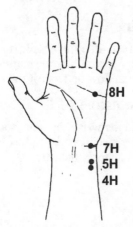
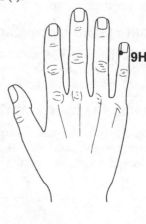

The Small intestine PM

Polarity:	Yang
Partner meridian:	Heart PM
Element:	Fire
Season:	Summer
Colour:	Red
Situation:	South
Organic tissue:	Arteries
Organic function:	Digestion, assimilation
Psychic energy:	Strength, fatigue, brilliant mind, neurasthenia
Energy peak:	Between 1 pm and 3 pm

Physiology of the Small intestine

The second phase of digestion takes place in the small intestine. The small intestine is a long pipe, about 6.4 metres long, in which digestion continues at a slower rate and whose purpose is to reduce foodstuffs into such small particles that they can cross the walls of the small intestine. This phase is known as assimilation.

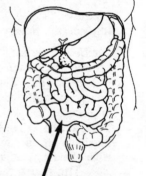

The physiology of Small intestine PM energy

The Small intestine

In some of the most ancient writings ever found, it is said that the small intestine is responsible for separating the pure from the impure. We must not forget that the cells of the small intestine must be sufficiently intelligent to allow nutrients favourable to our cells to cross their walls and to bar the way to unwanted and damaging substances. We can therefore conclude that the Heart Emperor is associated with the intelligence of the small intestine and this is why point 3SI, which boosts the Small intestine PM is also the Key point of the Governing Vessel which runs through the whole central nervous system, ie, down the length of the spine from the head.

The route taken by the Small intestine PM

The Small intestine PM starts at the corner of the little fingernail, runs up the cubital side of the hand, the forearm and the upper arm before running across the shoulder-blade and the neck and ending in a hollow up against the tragus.

Pain along the course of the Small intestine PM

The little finger, the ulna side of the hand and the wrist (the ulna is a bone in the forearm, on the same side as the little finger, whereas the radius is on the thumb side), the arm, the shoulder, the neck, the cheek, the ear.

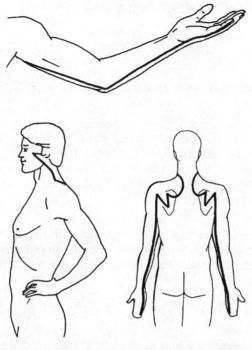

The route taken by the Small intestine PM

What to do if you feel pain along the course of the Small intestine PM

Boost the Ting point on both sides   1SI+
Boost the Booster point on the same side as the pain   4SI+
Replace by point 3SI in summer
Disperse the points surrounding the pain   –
Boost the Meeting point on both sides   13GB+

Symptoms of an energy excess in the Small intestine PM

Colic, loud laughter, extravagance.

How to disperse the Small intestine PM

In spring: 4SI-   In autumn: 2SI-
In summer: 8SI-   In winter: 3SI-
At the end of summer: 1SI-

Symptoms of an energy deficiency in the Small intestine PM

Difficulty in recovering after an effort, shiny and greasy stools, faulty assimilation.

How to boost the Small intestine PM

In spring:	2SI+	In autumn:	8SI+
In summer:	3SI	In winter:	1SI+
End of summer:	5SI+		

The most important points on the Small intestine PM

1SI: *Ting point*
Located at the corner of the little fingernail, on the ulna side of the hand.
This point boosts the Small intestine meridian in winter and disperses it at
the end of summer. In all seasons, it can treat the following disorders: When
boosted (+), this point reduces secretions and when dispersed (-), it
increases them (sweating, menstruation, lactation, seborrhoea).
Excessive sweating (+).
Hot flushes (-).

2SI: Located on the ulna edge of the hand, just before the joint.
This point boosts the Small intestine meridian in spring and disperses it in
autumn. In all seasons, it can treat the following disorders:
Nosebleeds (-).
Sore throat (-).
Buzzing in the ears (-).
Torticollis (-).

3SI: *Key point on the Governing Extraordinary Vessel*, which follows the spine.
Located just after the metacarpal/phalanx joint, opposite the crease formed
when the hand is closed.
This point boosts the Small intestine meridian during its season – summer
– and disperses it in winter. In all seasons, it can treat the following
disorders:
Backache along the spine (-).
Torticollis (-).
To recover after an effort (+).
To treat eye disorders and ear troubles, when combined with points 5TH
(-) and 41GB (-).

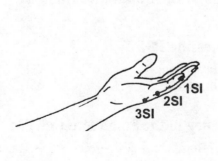

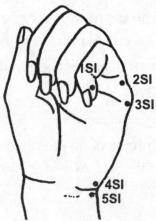

4SI: *Source point*
Located on the ulna edge of the hand, in a small hollow just before the wrist joint.
Very useful for replacing point 3SI in winter and spring.
To fight listlessness and lack of energy (+).
Stiffness or arthritis in the fingers or the wrist (-).
Headaches (-).
Buzzing in the ears (-).

5SI: Located in the hollow, just below point 4SI, on the other side of the joint. This point boosts the Small intestine meridian at the end of summer and disperses it in spring. In all seasons, it can treat the following disorders:
To stimulate circulation in the arteries (+).
To help thin people gain weight (+).
Buzzing in the ears (-).

8SI: Located behind the elbow, on the inside, ie, in the groove between the olecranon and ulna. This point disperses the Small intestine meridian in its season – summer – and boosts it in autumn. Pain in the shoulder, the shoulder-blade, the arm, and even spreading to the little finger.

18SI: Located on the face, below the hinge of the jawbone.
To stimulate the cheek muscles (+).

19SI: Located in a hollow up against the tragus. Has a beneficial action on disorders affecting the hearing.
Sudden deafness (+).
Buzzing in the ears (-).
Earache (-).

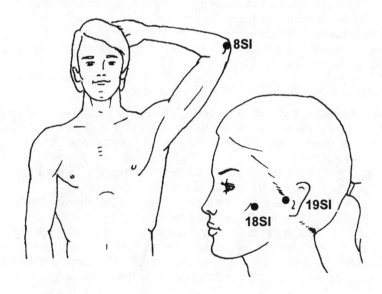

The Bladder Principal Meridian

Polarity:	Yang
Partner meridian:	Kidney PM
Element:	Water
Season:	Winter
Colour:	Black
Situation:	North
Organic tissue:	Bones and teeth
Organic function:	Elimination, cleansing
Psychic energy:	Courage, character, authority
Energy peak:	Between 3 pm and 5 pm

Physiology of the Bladder

The bladder is a reservoir in the shape of a funnel. Many layers of muscle form its wall and allow it to stretch to store urine from the kidneys until it is relieved by micturation.

The bladder can contain more than half a litre of urine. It flows into the bladder along the two ureters from the kidneys; one-way valves prevent it from returning to the kidneys. The urethra leaves the lower end of the bladder, which measures about 20 cm in an adult male, to conduct urine outside the body. The urethra is far shorter in women, which explains the greater occurrence of bladder disorders in women.

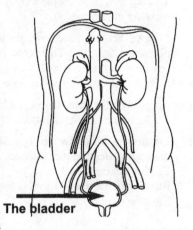

The bladder

In men, the prostate is situated at the base of the bladder and surrounds the first part of the urethra.

The physiology of Bladder PM energy

This is the largest meridian in the body. It is also the most 'yang' and because of this, it is most often in demand because it is linked with the most frequent disorders, in other words backache, headaches, nervousness, cramp in the calves, haemorrhoids, fungi, parasites, nose disorders, tear gland and genito-urinary troubles. Along with its partner meridian, the Kidney PM and the adrenal glands, it controls the energy of bravery.

We know that, among the hormones elaborated by the adrenal glands, adrenalin will increase our strength and our bravery when we are faced with danger. If there is an energy deficiency at this level, the subject will not be brave and will have trouble making decisions, whereas an individual who has an excess of this energy will make hasty decisions and possibly take unnecessary risks; he will definitely not lack courage and may be rather too authoritative!

The route taken by the Bladder PM

The Bladder PM starts at the inner corner of the eye, runs over the head, 1 fingerbreadth to either side of the central line, runs down the neck, the back and the buttocks, on down the leg, the outer edge of the feet and ends at the outer corner of the little toenail.

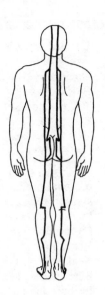

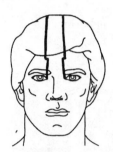

Pain along the course of the Bladder PM

A prickling sensation or pain at the inner corner of the eye, headaches, backache, cervical arthrosis, back pain, lumbago, sciatica, cramp in the calves, along the outer edge of the foot, the Achilles' tendon, the heel and the small toe.

What to do if you feel pain along the course of the Bladder PM

Boost the Ting point on both sides	67B+
Boost the Source point on the same side as the pain	64B+
Disperse the points surrounding the pain	–
Boost the Meeting point on both sides	2S+

Symptoms of an energy excess in the Bladder PM

Cystitis, inflammation of the bladder, of the ureter or of the prostate.

How to disperse the Bladder PM in the case of excess energy

In spring:	60B-	In autumn:	66B-
In summer:	54B-	In winter:	65B-
End of summer:	67B-		

Symptoms of an energy deficiency in the Bladder PM

Micturation more than 6 times a day, shyness, incontinence, parasites.

How to boost the Bladder PM in the event of deficiency

In spring:	66B+	In autumn:	54B+
In summer:	65B+	In winter:	67B+
End of summer:	60B+		

The most important points on the Bladder PM

1B: Located at the inner corner of the eye.
Eye troubles (-).
Conjunctivitis (-).
Blocked nose (-), combined with points 63B (-),
10B (-) and 3SI (-).
Aching forehead when the subject leans forward (-).
Excessive sweating (+).
Hot flushes (-).

10B: Located at the nape of the neck, below the
occipital protuberances. Acts on the para-
sympathetic nervous system.
Sweaty hands (-).
Hypersalivation (-).
Vertigo (-).
Neck pain (-).
Blocked nose at night (-).
Introversion (-).
Enuresia (-).

N.B.: All the following points, that is to say, from
11B to 26B, are 2 fingerbreadths to either
side of the spine, in the muscular groove.
They are usually very sensitive, which
makes them easier to pinpoint.

11B: *Master point governing the bones*
Located level with the first thoracic vertebra. Helps balance the Conception
and Governing Extraordinary Vessels.

12B: *Master point governing the nose*
Located level with the second and third thoracic vertebrae.
Sneezing (-).
Hay fever (-).
Nosebleeds (-).
Sinusitis (-).

13B: *Lu point for the lungs*
Located level with the third and fourth tho-
racic vertebrae.
To avoid catching influenza (+, as soon as
the first symptoms are felt)
Bronchitis (-).
Dry cough (+).
Sinusitis (+).

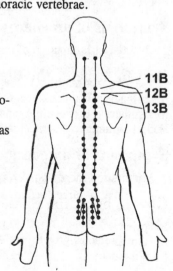

14B: *Lu point on the Master of the Heart*
Located level with the fourth and fifth thoracic vertebrae.
High blood pressure (-).
Heart pain (-).

15B: *Lu point for the Heart*
Located level with the fifth and sixth thoracic vertebrae.
Nervous heart pain (-).
Nerves (+).
Anxiety (+).
Anguish (+).
Palpitations (-).
People who tend to chatter about nothing (-).

16B: *Lu point on the Governing Vessel*
Located level with the sixth and seventh thoracic vertebrae.
Paralysis (+).
Tiredness (+).
Colic (-).
Flatulence (-).

17B: *Lu point governing the diaphragm muscle and the blood*
Located level with the seventh and eighth thoracic vertebrae.
Haemorrhage (+), combined
with point 9L (-).
Hiccups (-).

N.B.:   There is a space between
points 17B and 18B. This is
usually where a woman's bra
strap lies, so it can be used to
help you locate these points.
The tip of the shoulder-blade
can also be used to position
yourself since point 17B is
slightly above a horizontal
line drawn between these two
tips, whereas point 18B is 2
fingerbreadths below this
horizontal line, level with the
space between the ninth and
tenth thoracic vertebrae.

18B: *Lu point governing the Liver*
Located level with the ninth
and tenth thoracic vertebrae.
Has a direct action on the
liver, the eyes and the muscles.
Promotes growth in children
(+).

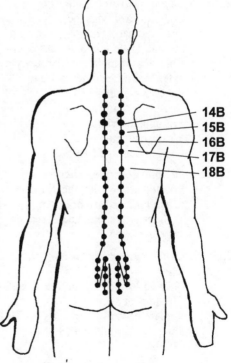

14B
15B
16B
17B
18B

19B: *Lu point governing the Gall-Bladder*
Located level with the tenth and eleventh thoracic vertebrae. Acts directly on the gall-bladder, migraine, feelings of nausea, dry and bitter taste in the mouth, irritability.

20B: *Lu point governing the Spleen and the Pancreas*
Located above the ribs, level with the eleventh and twelfth thoracic vertebrae. Acts on a swollen and painful tummy or diarrhoea.
Precaution: Avoid stimulating this point in insulin-dependent diabetics since overintensive stimulation can provoke a coma.

21B: *Lu point governing the Stomach*
Located beneath the twelfth rib.
Lazy stomach (+).
Slow digestion (+).
Stomach cramps or heartburn (-).

22B: *Lu point governing the Triple Heater*
Located level with the first and second lumbar vertebrae.
To stimulate digestion (+).
Insomnia due to oversensitive lower members (-).
Enuresia (+), combined with point 23B (+).

23B: *Lu point governing the Kidneys*
Located level with the second and third lumbar vertebrae. Very important, since this point is responsible for stimulating the body's defences and lending courage.
Excessive diuresia (+).
Nocturnal diuresia (+).
Morning diarrhoea (+).
Weak sexuality (+).
Lack of courage (+).

24B: *Lu point governing energy*
Located level with the third and fourth lumbar vertebrae.
To increase general and sexual energy level (+).

25B: *Lu point governing the Large intestine*
Located level with the fourth and fifth lumbar vertebrae.
Straightforward diarrhoea (+).
Sluggish constipation (+).
Colitis (-).
Constipation due to spasms (-).
Diarrhoea due to inflammation (-).

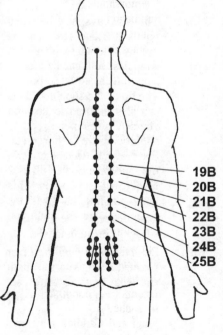

19B
20B
21B
22B
23B
24B
25B

26B: *Lu point governing the Conception Vessel*
Located level with the sacro-iliac joint. Has a beneficial action on painful periods and diarrhoea.

27B: *Lu point governing the Small intestine*
Located 2 fingerbreadths outside the first sacral hollow. Treats diarrhoea, enteritis and colitis. Incontinence (+), combined with point 28B (+).

28B: *Lu point governing the Bladder*
Located 2 fingerbreadths outside the second sacral hollow.
Abundant urine (+).
Cystitis (-).
Inflammation of the genital organs (-).
Haemorrhoids (-).
Water retention (-).
Frequent but insufficient urination (-).

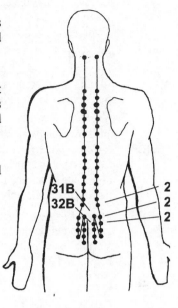

31B: Located in the first sacral hollow.
Gynaecological disorders and affections (-).
Hot flushes (-).
Haemorrhoids (-).
Lumbago (-).
Sciatica (-).
Soothes the pain of contractions during birth (-).

32B: Located in the second sacral hollow. Completes the action of point 31B.

38B: Located against the shoulder-blade, level with the fourth intercostal space.
Increases the number of red blood cells (+).
Increases energy (-).
Fights anorexia, neurasthenia, chronic bronchitis and vertigo (+).

54B: Located right in the centre of the back of the knee. This point disperses the Bladder meridian in summer and boosts it in autumn. In all seasons, it can treat the following disorders:
Dry skin (+).
Dry hair (+).
Eczema (+), combined with points 13B (-) and 60B (-).
Backache (-).
Fungi and Candida albicans (-), combined with points 67B (+), 5Sp (+) and 3Sp (-).

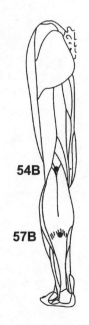

57B: *Master point governing haemorrhoids*
Located below the calf muscle.
Haemorrhoids (-).
Cramp (-).

58B: *Lo point*
Located in a small hollow on the outer, rear side of the leg, behind the fibula, 5 fingerbreadths above point 60B which is behind the lateral malleolus. To stimulate the leg muscles (+).
Sciatica (-).
Cramp in the leg muscles (-).

60B: *Sedative point for pain*
Located behind the lateral malleolus. This point boosts the Bladder meridian at the end of summer and disperses it in spring. Disperse it for any type of pain. This is the only point that can be dispersed during menstruation (-).

62B: *Major Key point for treating a general excess of yang*
Located below the lateral malleolus.
Vertical back pain (-).
Insomnia (-).
Acne (-).
Nervousness (-).
Fear of the dark (+).

64B: *Source point*
Located on the outer edge of the foot, in front of the fifth metatarsal joint.
Incontinence (+).
Cystitis (-).
Urinary inflammation (-).
Inflammation of the prostate gland (-).

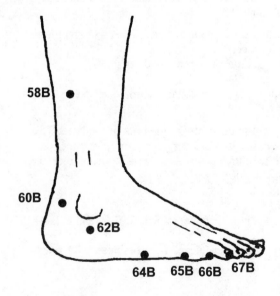

65B: Located on the outer edge of the foot, just before the small toe joint.
This point disperses the Bladder meridian in its season – winter – and boosts
it in summer. In all seasons, it can treat the following disorders:
Cystitis (-).
Inflammation of the urinary passages (-).
Acne on the back (-).

66B: Located just after the small toe joint.
This point boosts the Bladder meridian in spring and disperses it in autumn.
In all seasons, it can treat the following disorders:
Blocked nose (-).
Dizziness (-).
Sensitive eyes (-).

67B: *Ting point*
Located at the outer corner of the small toenail.
This point boosts the Bladder meridian in its season – winter – and disperses
it at the end of summer. In all seasons, it can treat the following disorders:
Repositions the foetus in its correct position (+).
Incontinence (+).
Blocked nose (+).
Sinusitis (+).
Athlete's foot (+).
Intestinal parasites (+, during the full moon and new moon)
Back pain (+).

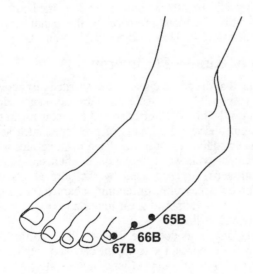

The Kidney PM

Polarity:	Yin
Partner meridian:	Bladder PM
Element:	Water
Season:	Winter
Colour:	Black
Situation:	North
Organic tissue:	Bones, teeth, ears
Organic function:	Filtering, elimination
Psychic energy:	Courage, decision
Energy peak:	Between 5 pm and 7 pm

Physiology of the Kidneys

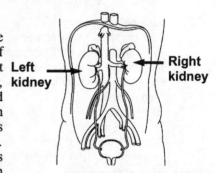

The kidneys filter the blood. The kidneys can be viewed as a mesh of selective fibres whose purpose is to let undesirable elements pass through – urea, acids, waste contained in the blood – and to prevent our mineral salts from escaping. It is estimated that the kidneys filter about 2000 litres of blood every day. Only 1.5 litres of urine are excreted. This role as a filter prevents the accumulation of waste that can damage our health. The kidneys are also involved in regulating our blood pressure, by adjusting the amount of water in the body. They produce hormones that help control the blood pressure and the manufacture of red blood corpuscles in the bone marrow. They also activate vitamin D.

The physiology of Kidney PM energy

We must not forget that the adrenal glands are situated just above the kidneys and that they are responsible for secreting adrenalin and adrenal cortical hormones. Adrenalin is the bravery hormone and corticoids help the body fight against any aggressions and avoid all sorts of problems, such as rheumatism. Levels of potassium and sodium are also regulated by mineralocorticoids, hence the kidneys' involvement with water retention or diuresis. Sexual hormones (androgens and oestrogens) are produced by the adrenal glands, and these substances can reinforce the masculine or feminine character traits in individuals. Ancient writings have always attached great importance to the link between the kidneys and sexuality and virility.

The Kidney PM belongs – as does the Bladder PM – to the element Water which is connected with the bones, the teeth, the ears and with mineral salts (the greatest concentration of mineral salts is found in sea water).

An energy deficiency in the kidneys can cause decalcification, arthrosis or rheumatism. The subject will be liable to have difficulty making decisions, will lack courage, and the cold and fear will cause him to urinate. Individuals with an excess of this energy, however, will be very brave, will often take unnecessary risks and will tend to be bossy.

The route taken by the Kidney PM

The Kidney PM starts under the foot then runs up behind the inner ankle, the leg, the inner side of the thigh, the groin, the abdomen and the thorax, 1 fingerbreadth to each side of the median line, to end on each side of the breastbone, below the clavicle.

Pain along the course of the Kidney PM

Pain on the sole of the foot, the heel, the inner ankle, the inside of the leg, the thigh, the groin, the abdomen or the thorax, along the course of the meridian.

What to do if you feel pain along the course of the Kidney PM

Boost the Ting point on both sides	1K+
Boost the Booster point on the same side as the pain	7K+
Disperse the points surrounding the pain	–
Boost the Meeting point	3CV+

Symptoms of an energy excess in the Kidney PM

Urination less than 4 times a day, dark urine, taking exaggerated risks, excessive authority, nephritis (kidney inflammation), uric lithiasis, kidney infections.

How to disperse the Kidney PM in the event of excess energy

In spring:	2K-	In autumn:	10K-
In summer:	3K-	In winter:	1K-
End of summer:	7K-		

Symptoms of an energy deficiency in the Kidney PM

Urination more than 6 times a day, morning diarrhoea, a feeling of being chilled to the bone, indecision, unjustified fears.

How to boost the Kidney PM in the event of energy deficiency

In spring:	10K+	In autumn:	3K+
In summer:	1K+	In winter:	7K+
End of summer:	2K+		

The most important points on the Kidney PM

1K: *Ting point*
Resuscitation point
Located on the sole of the foot, between the two muscle masses.
This point disperses the Kidney meridian in its season – winter – and boosts it in summer. In all seasons, it can treat the following disorders:
A faint (+).
Urine retention (-).
Uraemia (-).
Albuminuria (-).
Convulsions (-).
Epilepsy (-).
High blood pressure (-).

2K: Located 2 fingerbreadths above the medial malleolus, below the end of the navicular (which is prominent).
This point boosts the Kidney meridian at the end of summer and disperses it in spring. In all seasons, it can treat the following disorders:
High blood pressure (-).
Bruising (-).
Congestion in the lower abdomen (-).

3K: *Source point*
Located just behind the medial malleolus.
This point disperses the Kidney meridian in its season – winter – and boosts it in autumn. In all seasons, it can treat the following disorders:
Rheumatism (+).
People who are too thin (+).
Fearful people (+).

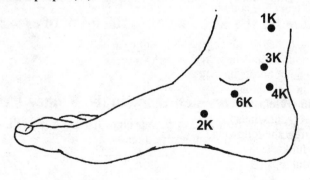

4K: *Lo point*
Located 2 fingerbreadths above point 3K, slightly to the rear, in other words on the upper edge of the calcaneus, in front of the Achilles' tendon.
This point is effective in treating certain cases of lumbago. Subjects who are oversensitive to cold (+).
Subjects who fear draughts (+).
Indecisive individuals (+).
Fearful people (+).
Renal colic (-).
Shyness, fear (+).

6K: *Key point on the Yin Keo EV*
Located below the medial malleolus.
Insomnia (+), combined with point 62B (-).
Sleepiness (-).
PMT (-).
Tender breasts before periods (-).
Cystitis (-).
Urethritis (-).
Cramp (-).
Nocturnal epileptic fits (-).
Nocturnal cramp (-).

7K: Located 2 fingerbreadths above the medial malleolus, in front of the Achilles' tendon.
This point boosts the Kidney meridian in its season – winter – and disperses it in summer. In all seasons, it can treat the following disorders:
To increase the excretion of urinary waste and reduce the quantity of urine, which will become darker (+).
To help fight bouts of rheumatism (+).
To stimulate the body's defence system (+).
To stimulate the adrenal glands (+).
Excessive urination, particularly at night (+).
Fearful people (+).
Perpetually dissatisfied people (+).
Diminished hearing (-).
Tendency to suffer from arthrosis and dental caries (+).
Cold feet (+), combined with point 32S (-).

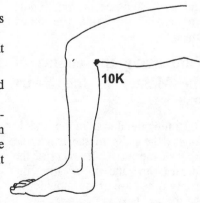

10K: Located below the crease formed when the knee is bent.
This point boosts the Kidney meridian in spring and disperses it in autumn. Helps reduce cellulite in the knees (-, in winter) In all seasons, it can treat the following disorders:
Painful knees (-).
Painful hips (-).

The Master of the Heart PM

Polarity:	Yin
Partner meridian:	Triple Heater PM
Element:	Fire
Season:	Summer
Colour:	Pink
Situation:	South
Organic tissue:	Pericardium
Organic function:	Vasoconstriction
Psychic energy:	Sentimentality, emotionalism, sexuality, interior nervousness
Energy peak:	Between 7 pm and 9 pm

Physiology of the Master of the Heart PM energy

The Master of the Heart meridian corresponds both to the heart's nervous system and the blood vessel system. It therefore plays a part in vasomotricity. The Master of the Heart is also connected with sexuality. Physically, it corresponds to the pericardium, which envelops the heart and psychologically, it corresponds to the protective envelope sheltering us from emotional influence. This meridian must be stimulated to treat pain close to the heart, or spasms and palpitations caused by distress.

There are various points used for calming spasms in the solar plexus, the stomach or the heart, due to stress (6MH); for reducing or increasing the blood pressure (7MH and 9MH); to stimulate sexuality (8MH) and to combat blushing due to emotion (6MH and 7MH).

The route taken by the Master of the Heart PM

The Master of the Heart PM starts on the thorax in the region of the heart, just next to the nipple, runs across the top of the armpit and down the front of the arm, the forearm, the wrist and the hand, to end at the corner of the middle fingernail, alongside the index finger.

Pain along the course of the Master of the Heart PM

Pain or numbness in the middle finger, the palm of the hand, the front of the wrist, the front of the forearm and the upper arm, the front of the base of the shoulder or the thorax, next to the breast.

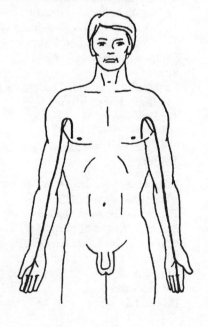

What to do if you feel pain along the course of the Master of the Heart PM

Boost the Ting point on both sides	9MH+
Boost the Booster point on the same side as the pain	7MH+
	except in summer
Disperse the points surrounding the pain	–
Boost the Meeting point on both sides	22GB+

Symptoms of an energy excess in the Master of the Heart PM

High blood pressure (particularly the systolic value), tachycardia, writer's cramp, nymphomania.

How to disperse the Master of the Heart PM in the event of excess energy

In spring:	8MH	In autumn:	3MH-
In summer:	7MH-	In winter:	9MH-
End of summer:	5MH-		

Symptoms of an energy deficiency in the Master of the Heart PM

Low blood pressure, dizziness, depression, pessimism.

How to boost the Master of the Heart PM in the event of energy deficiency

In spring:	3MH+	In autumn:	7MH+
In summer:	9MH+	In winter:	5MH+
End of summer:	8MH+		

The most important points on the Master of the Heart PM

3MH: Located in the crease of the elbow, next to the inner edge of the biceps tendon.
This point boosts the Master of the Heart meridian in spring and disperses it in autumn. In all seasons, it can treat the following disorders:
Pessimism (-).
Fever due to a chill (-).
Measles (-).

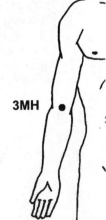

3MH

5MH: Located 3 fingerbreadths below the crease of the elbow, on the inside.
This point boosts the Master of the Heart meridian in winter and disperses
it at the end of summer. In all seasons, it can treat the following disorders:
Emotionalism (-).
Hypersalivation (-).
Swelling in the armpit (-).
Convulsions in children (-).

6MH: *Lo point*
Key point on the Yin Oe Extraordinary Vessel
Located 3 fingerbreadths above the crease formed when the wrist is bent
forward, between the two tendons.
To calm spasms in various organs (-).
Internal nervous pain (-).
Emotionalism (-).
Pain in the region of the heart (-).
Anxiety (-)
Insomnia in subjects who tend to internalise their feelings (-).
Inflammation of the arteries (-).
Hiccups (-).

7MH: *Source point*
Located in the centre of the crease on the inside of the wrist.
This point disperses the Master of the Heart meridian in its season – summer
– and boosts it in autumn. In all seasons, it can treat the following disorders:
To reduce blood pressure, particularly the systolic value (-).
Cramp in the hand (-).
Pain in the fingers and the forearm (-).
Palpitations (-).
Agitation (-).
Internal nervousness (-).

8MH: *Seasonal point on the Master of the Heart PM in summer*
Located right in the centre of the palm of the hand, on the crease that crosses
the heart line.
This point disperses the Master of the Heart meridian in spring and boosts
it at the end of summer. In all seasons, it can treat the following disorders:
Weak sexuality (+).
Lack of good humour (+).
High blood pressure (-).
Nauseous migraine (-), combined with points 40GB (-) and 3Lv (-).

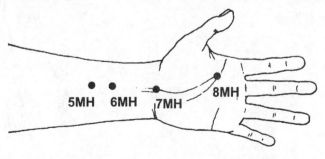

9MH: *Ting point*
Located at the corner of the middle fingernail, alongside the index finger.
This point boosts the Master of the Heart meridian in its season – summer
– and disperses it in winter. In all seasons, except winter, it can treat the
folloiwng disorders:
Low blood pressure (+).
Extreme lassitude (+).
Children who cry at night (+).

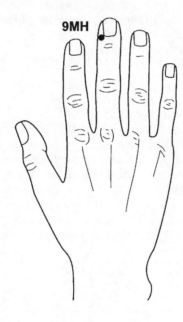

The Triple Heater PM

Polarity:	Yang
Partner meridian:	Master of the Heart PM
Element:	Fire
Season:	Summer
Colour:	Red
Situation:	South
Organic tissue:	Non-existent since this is a function
Organic function:	Thermoregulation
Psychic energy:	Excitement, dynamism, externalisation
Energy peak:	Between 9 pm and 11 pm

Physiology of the Triple Heater PM energy

This meridian is not connected with an organ but with a specific function: it stores the energy produced by the functioning of all our organs, before distributing it according to the body's requirements, in three main areas:

Upper level: in the region of the head and the cardio-respiratory system.

Middle level: below the diaphragm, in the region of the digestive system.

Lower level: corresponds to the functions of elimination and fertilisation. (It is not by chance that the end coincides with the beginning of life and the reproductive system.)

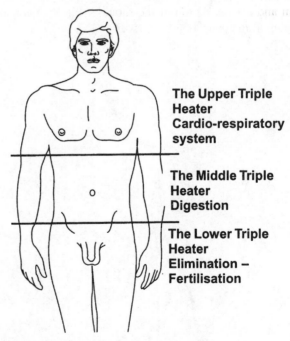

The Upper Triple Heater Cardio-respiratory system

The Middle Triple Heater Digestion

The Lower Triple Heater Elimination – Fertilisation

The 3 levels of the Triple Heater PM

The Triple Heater is a very yang meridian. It features in the Fire element which represents heat and dynamism. Subjects suffering from a Triple Heater energy deficiency will feel the cold and will lack stamina.

Quite the opposite is true of individuals who have an excess of Triple Heater energy; they will literally sparkle with life; they are always ready to enjoy themselves, they enjoy eating, drinking and being merry and are quite likely to 'burn the candle at both ends'. They are often hot-blooded and have a highly coloured complexion. They also tend to suffer from high blood pressure.

Between an excess resulting in overexternalisation and an energy deficiency which means subjects feel the cold, internalise their feelings and lack human warmth, there is plenty of space for finding a fair balance. Individuals who are well-balanced – from the Triple Heater meridian point of view – will be sufficiently dynamic to make the most of the joys of life without 'going overboard' and indulging in dangerous pleasures. This is why it is so important to stabilise this meridian, to protect our heart and blood vessels, thus preserving our life, avoiding burning it inconsiderately but maintaining a decent flame to warm the heart and the mind.

There is a Booster point and a Source point on this meridian, which lend heat and vitality to those who need it, and a Dispersion point to quieten overexcited subjects.

The route taken by the Triple Heater PM

The Triple Heater PM starts at the corner of the fourth fingernail, alongside the little finger, runs up the back of the hand, the wrist, the forearm, the upper arm and across the top of the shoulder, up the neck and round the ear before ending at the outer tip of the eyebrow.

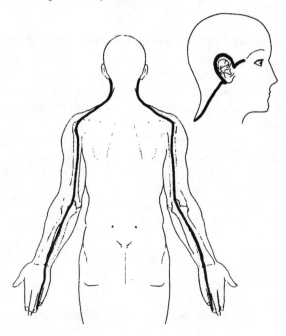

What to do if you feel pain along the course of the Triple Heater PM

Boost the Ting point on both sides	1TH+
Boost the Booster point on the same side as the pain	4TH+
Disperse the points surrounding the pain	–
Boost the Meeting point on both sides	13GB+

Symptoms of an energy excess in the Triple Heater PM

Thermophobia, redness, excitement, loud voice, tendency to 'burn the candle at both ends'.

How to disperse the Triple Heater PM in the event of excess energy

In spring:	6TH-	In autumn:	2TH-
In summer:	10TH-	In winter:	3TH-
End of summer:	1TH-		

Symptoms of an energy deficiency in the Triple Heater PM

The subject feels the cold, lacks vitality and is pale.

How to boost the Triple Heater PM in the event of energy deficiency

In spring:	2TH+	In autumn:	10TH+
In summer:	3TH+	In winter:	1TH+
End of summer:	6TH+		

The most important points on the Triple Heater PM

1TH: *Ting point*
Located at the corner of the fourth fingernail, alongside the little finger. This point disperses the Triple Heater meridian at the end of summer and boosts it in winter. In all seasons, it can treat the following disorders:
Dry mouth (-).
Pain along the course of the meridian (+).

2TH: Located between the fourth and little fingers, just before the joint. Boosts the Triple Heater PM in spring and disperses it in autumn. In all seasons, it can treat the following disorders:
Buzzing in the ears or sudden deafness (-).
Headaches when the weather is bad (-).
Stiff and painful neck (-).

3TH: Located between the fourth and fifth metacarpals, just below the joint. This point boosts the Triple Heater in its season – summer – and disperses it at the end of summer. In all seasons, it can treat the following disorders:
To stimulate thermoregulation (+).
If the subject is sad, discouraged, fed up with life, depressed (+).

4TH: *Source point*
Located on the crease on the back of the wrist.
Painful wrist (-).
Feeling the cold (+).
To increase vigour (+).
To quieten overexcited individuals (-).
To stimulate the extender muscles of the hand (+).

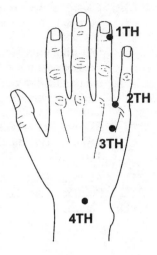

5TH: *Key point on the Yang Oe Extraordinary Vessel*
Lo point on the Triple Heater PM
Located 2 fingerbreadths above the crease on the back of the wrist when it is bent, in between the 2 bones of the forearm.
Pain in the joints due to a weather change (-).
Headache after being out in the sun (-).
Ear problems: sudden deafness, earache, buzzing in the ears (-).
Cramp in the muscles of the hand (-).

6TH: Located 3 fingerbreadths above the crease on the back of the wrist when it is bent, between the 2 bones of the forearm.
This point boosts the Triple Heater meridian at the end of summer and disperses it in spring. In all seasons, it can treat the following disorders:
Constipation (-).
Pain in the shoulder (-).
Acne (-).

8TH: *Lo point of the 3 Yang PMs in the upper members*
Analgesia point in acupuncture
Located 5 fingerbreadths above the crease on the back of the wrist when it is bent, between the 2 bones of the forearm.
Pain in the shoulders (-).
Torticollis (-).
Pain along the outer side of the forearm and the upper arm (-).
Dyshidrosis (-).

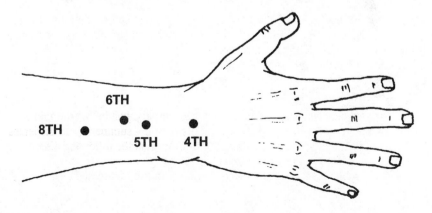

10TH: Located above the tip of the olecranon, ie, in the hollow behind the elbow. This point disperses the Triple Heater meridian in its season – summer – and boosts it in autumn. In all seasons, except autumn, it can treat the following disorders:

Nervousness (-).

Interior tension (-).

Agitation (-).

Difficulty in falling asleep (-).

Excessive externalisation (-).

High blood pressure (-), combined with points 7H (-), 7MH (-) and 6Sp (-).

Torticollis (-).

17TH: All located in the little hollows around the back of the ear.
18TH: Buzzing in the ears (-), combined with 5TH (-).
19TH: Earache (-), combined with 5TH.
20TH:

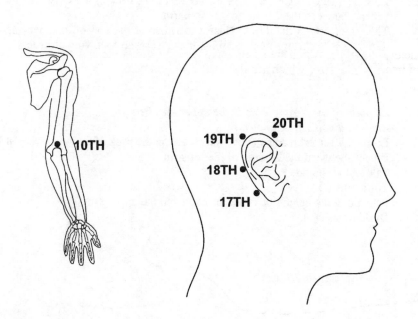

The Gall-Bladder PM

Polarity:	Yang
Partner meridian:	Liver PM
Element:	Wood
Season:	Spring
Colour:	Green
Situation:	East
Organic tissue:	Muscles, eyes
Organic function:	Digestion
Psychic energy:	Combat, aggressiveness, defence, performance
Energy peak:	Between 11 pm and 1 am

Physiology of the Gall-Bladder

The gall-bladder is a sac that collects the bile produced by the liver (about 1 litre per day). It then empties the bile into the first section of the small intestine, the duodenum. Bile neutralises the acidity of the bolus of food as it leaves the stomach and thus allows digestion to continue in an alkaline environment. It also plays a vital part in the digestion of fats. Bile contains no digestive enzymes but it does allow the pancreatic enzymes to complete the digestion of starch, which begins in the mouth. Bile contains bilirubin (which gives it its colour), lecithin, cholesterol and bile salts. Accumulations of these substances can form 'stones'. There are three types: cholesterol stones which can reach more than 1 cm in diameter, bile stones which are smaller and far more common, and mixed stones of an intermediate size, which are the most common type.

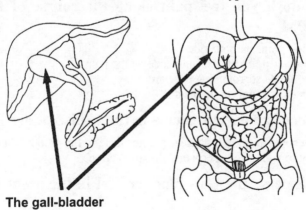

The gall-bladder

The physiology of Gall-Bladder PM energy

From an energy point of view, the Liver and Gall-bladder meridians produce 'combat energy'. We must not forget that life is a constant battle against bad habits, preconceived ideas, laziness, germs, bacteria, viruses, fungi, negative weather conditions (too windy, too hot, too cold, too dry, too humid), but also, and most important, psychological disorders, stress and worry. Therefore, it is not at all surprising to find points that diffuse anger (40GB), calm nervousness (20GB), a master point governing muscles (34GB) and a point to increase assertiveness, all situated along the Gall-bladder meridian.

The route taken by the Gall-Bladder PM

The Gall-bladder PM starts at the outer corner of the eye, runs across the side of the skull, the neck, the trunk, the outside of the thigh and the leg to end at the corner of the fourth toenail, alongside the small toe.

Pain along the course of the Gall-Bladder PM

Sensitivity disorders, malformation or pain in the fourth toe, the foot, the ankle (swelling like an egg in front of and below the lateral malleolus), the outside of the leg along the fibula where one can feel a burning sensation (too much yang) or numbness (too much yin), the outside of the thigh along the femur, the hip (arthritis etc), pain on the side of the ribs, the shoulder (like a strap), along the side of the neck, migraine in the temple, at the outer edge of the eye, in the occipital region (at the back of the head).

What to do if you feel pain along the course of the Gall-Bladder PM

Boost the Ting point on both sides	44GB+
Boost the Booster point on the same side as the pain	40GB+
Disperse the points surrounding the pain	–
Boost the Meeting point on both sides	2S+

Symptoms of an energy excess in the Gall-Bladder PM

Vindictiveness, migraine, nausea, a bitter taste in the mouth when you wake up, tendency to sigh often, perpetual dissatisfaction.

How to disperse the Gall-Bladder PM in the event of excess energy

In spring:	38GB-	In autumn:	43GB-
In summer:	34GB-	In winter:	41GB-
End of summer:	44GB-		

Symptoms of an energy deficiency in the Gall-Bladder PM

Insomnia because of apprehension, pain in the fourth toe, lack of assertiveness, tendency to procrastinate.

How to boost the Gall-Bladder PM in the event of energy deficiency

In spring:	43GB+	In autumn:	34GB+
In summer:	41GB+	In winter:	44GB+
End of summer:	38GB+		

The most important points on the Gall-Bladder PM

13GB: *Meeting point*
Situated right on the hairline, following a line from the corner of the outer eye. This point completes the treatment of pain on the route of the Triple Heater, Small intestine and the Large intestine meridians.

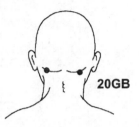

20GB: Located at the back of the neck, below the occipital protuberances.
This point is connected with the sympathetic nervous system.
Hot flushes with sweating (+).
Insufficient menstruation (+).
Headaches (-).
Hot flushes without sweating (-).
Fever without sweating (-).
Torticollis (-).
Nervousness (-).

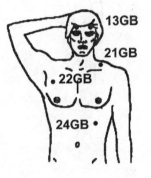

21GB: *Contusion point*
Resuscitation point
Located at the base of the neck, in the hollow behind the clavicle
Cysts or abscesses in the breasts (-).
Torticollis (-).

22GB: *Meeting point of the Heart, Master of the Heart and Lung meridians*
Situated at the side of the thorax, in the fourth intercostal space, below the armpit on the same level as a line across the upper part of the breast.

24GB: *Mo point governing the Gall-Bladder meridian*
Located in the space between the two lowest ribs, directly below the nipple.
This point governs the uterus and assists birth.
Lazy gall-bladder (+).
Vomiting (-).
Migraine (-).

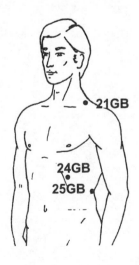

25GB: *Mo point governing the Kidneys*
Located at the end of the twelfth rib, which is the floating rib whose tip can be seen at the base of the thorax.
Overabundant urine (+).
Kidney pain (-), combined with point 4K (-) and 60B (-).
Morning diarrhoea (+).
Feeling chilled to the bone (+).
Loss of bone mineral (+).

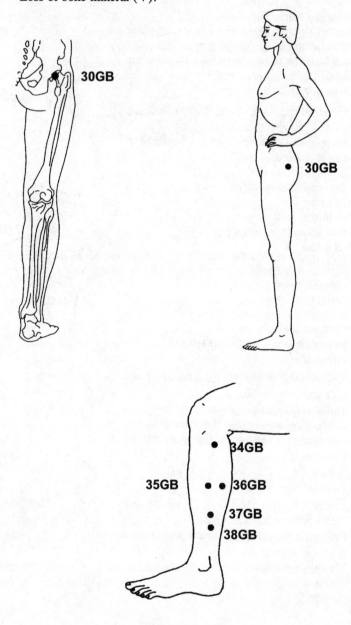

30GB: Located behind the greater trochanter which is the bony protuberance you can feel in the buttock, particularly when the leg is rotated.
Hip pain (-).
Migraine (-).
Itching (-), combined with 5Lv (+).
Rashes with fever (-).
Heavy hips (-).

34GB: *Master point governing striated muscle*
Located below the outer side of the knee, just below the head of the fibula, the small bony bump you can feel just below the knee, slightly to the rear. This point boosts the Gall-Bladder meridian in autumn and disperses it in summer. In all seasons, it can treat the following disorders:
Muscular weakness (+).
Cramp (-).
Stiff muscles (-).
To induce birth (-).

35GB: *Contusion point*
Located halfway down the lower leg, in front of or behind the fibula, depending on whose teachings you follow. To obtain maximum effect, stimulate both points.
Painful coccyx (-).
Cold feet (+).
Pain along the outside of the leg (-).

36GB: *This point should be stimulated to combat insect and animal venom*
Stimulate this point to cure infected wounds that refuse to heal
Located halfway down the lower leg, in front of or behind the fibula, depending on whose teachings you follow. To obtain maximum effect, stimulate both points.
Venomous insect sting or animal bites (-).
Infected wounds that refuse to heal (-).
Inflammation of the larynx (-).
Scoliosis (abnormal lateral curvature of the spine) (-).

37GB: *Lo point*
Major point governing the eyes
Located on the outside of the leg, 5 fingerbreadths above the lateral malleolus, in front of the fibula.
Eye disorders (-).
Nausea (-).
Palpitations (-).
Itching (-).
Numb feet (-).

38GB: Located 4 fingerbreadths above the lateral malleolus, in a small hollow on the front edge of the fibula.
This point disperses the Gall-Bladder meridian in its season – spring – and boosts it at the end of summer. In all seasons, it can treat the following disorders:

Migraine (-).
Nausea (-).
Bitter taste and dry mouth in the morning (-).
Dark shadows under the eyes (-).
Irritability and sensitivity (-).
Precaution: Avoid stimulating this point in subjects who suffer from gallstones because it provokes the contraction of the gall-bladder, encouraging the expulsion of stones which would risk the obstruction of the bile duct.

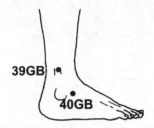

39GB: *Master point governing arteritis*
Located 2 fingerbreadths above the lateral malleolus, on the fibula.
Arteritis (+).
To encourage the healing of wounds (+).
Inflammation of the respiratory channels (-).
Dry throat and nose (-).
To increase the number of white blood cells (+).
To increase the body temperature in the case of infection and to accelerate recovery (+).
To cause abscesses to come to a head (+).

40GB: *Source point*
Located on the top of the foot, in a hollow just in front of the lateral malleolus.
Migraine (-).
Numbness (-).
Cramp in the calf muscles (-).
Pain in the armpit (-).
Lack of assertiveness (+).

41GB: *Key point on the Tae Mo Extraordinary vessel*
Located at the top of the angle formed by the fourth and fifth metatarsals. This point boosts the Gall-Bladder meridian in summer and disperses it in winter. In all seasons, it can treat the following disorders:
Horizontal back pain in the lumbar region (-).
Hip pain (-).
Trembling (-), combined with point 3MH (-).
Shoulder pain (-).
Sight disorders (-).
Lactation disorders (-).
Inflammation of the breasts (-), combined with point 21GB (-).

Rheumatism in the feet, heels, ankles, toes (-).
Buzzing or whistling in the ears (-).

43GB: Located between the last two toes.
This point boosts the Gall-Bladder meridian in its season – spring – and disperses it in autumn. In all seasons, it can treat the following disorders:
Lack of daring and assertiveness (+).
Dizziness (+).
Hazy sight (+).

44GB: *Ting point*
Located at the outer corner of the fourth toenail.
This point boosts the Gall-Bladder meridian in winter and disperses it at the end of summer. In all seasons, it can treat the following disorders:
Migraine (-).
Pain in the eye (-).
Sore throat (+).

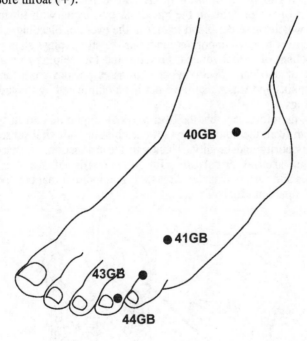

The Liver PM

Polarity:	Yin
Partner meridian:	Gall-Bladder PM
Element:	Wood
Season:	Spring
Colour:	Blue
Situation:	East
Organic tissue:	Muscles, eyes
Organic function:	Eliminating poisons
Psychic energy:	Combat, anger, anxiety
Energy peak:	Between 1 am and 3 am

Physiology of the Liver

The liver is the gland that contains the most blood in the human body. It can contain 1.5 litres of the 5 litres of blood spread round our body. The liver produces most of the proteins in the blood plasma, along with fibrinogen and prothrombin which cause the blood to clot in the event of bleeding.

In fact, the liver has two important functions. Firstly, it plays an imprtant role in the metabolism of carbohydrates, proteins and fat, helping to maintain the right balance of nutrients. Secondly, it eliminates poisons from the body by neutralising toxins and waste that have not been eliminated by the kidneys, the skin or the lungs.

One could, therefore, say that the liver plays an important part in controlling the blood, both from the point of view of enriching it with vital substances and in ensuring its purity and fluidity. Thanks to these functions, it maintains the quality of our arterial circulation. In other words, if we are to avoid atherosclerosis and cardio-vascular disease, it is important that our liver should be allowed to function efficiently.

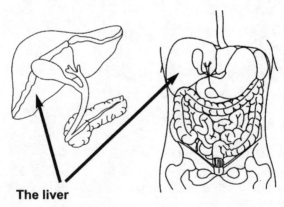

The liver

The physiology of Liver PM energy

In the Law of the 5 elements, the Liver meridian comes under the Wood element which is associated with spring, when green and blue predominate in nature. These are soothing colours. The best relaxation points are found on the Liver (3Lv) and Gall-Bladder (40GB) meridians. Just as wood purifies the atmosphere of the Earth, the liver purifies our body. Life is a constant battle against things that try to poison our existence (toxins, germs, stress). This is why points 8Lv and 14Lv can be just as useful in making individuals more assertive as in reducing the effects of a hangover.

The route taken by the Liver PM

The Liver PM starts at the outer corner of the big toenail, runs up the inside of the leg and thigh, across the groin and the abdomen to end on the thorax, below the breast.

Pain along the course of the Liver PM

Ingrown toenail on the big toe, painful big toe, pain on the upper side of the foot, the inside of the leg, the knee, the thigh and the side of the front of the trunk as far as just below the breast.

What to do if you feel pain along the course of the Liver PM

Boost the Ting point on both sides	1Lv+
Boost the booster point on the same side as the pain	8Lv+
in autumn, replace this point by 3Lv	
Disperse the points surrounding the pain	–
Boost the Meeting point on both sides	3CV+

Symptoms of an energy excess in the Liver PM

Yellow skin, tendency to fits of anger, aggressiveness, liver colic, exaggerated erections, poor eyesight in dim light.

How to disperse the Liver PM in the event of excess energy

In spring:	2Lv-	In autumn:	8Lv-
In summer:	3Lv-	In winter:	1Lv-
End of summer:	4Lv-		

Symptoms of an energy deficiency in the Liver PM

Anxiety, tendency to worry, yellow and grey stools, tendency to bruise easily, slow coagulation of the blood, difficulty in attaining an erection, premature ejaculation, allergies, poor sight.

How to boost the Liver PM in the event of energy deficiency

In spring:	8Lv+	In autumn:	3Lv+
In summer:	1Lv+	In winter:	4Lv+
End of summer:	2Lv+		

The most important points on the Liver PM

1Lv: *Ting point*
The Liver's seasonal point in spring
Located at the outer corner of the big toenail. This point boosts the Liver meridian in summer and disperses it in winter. In all seasons, it can treat the following disorders:
Promotes the liver's functioning in spring,
– if you like spring and the colour blue (+).
– if you don't like spring and the colour blue (-).
Pain in the region of the navel (+).
Incontinence (+).

2Lv: Located in between the first two toes. This point disperses the Liver meridian in its season – spring – and boosts it at the end of summer. In all seasons, it can treat the following disorders:
Anger (-).
Suicidal tendencies (-).
Spasms (-).
Liver colic (-).
Painful penis (-).
Hot flushes (-), combined with point 1SI (+).

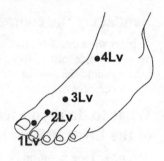

3Lv: *Source point*
Relaxation point
Located at the top of the angle formed by the first two metatarsals when the toes are spread.
This point boosts the Liver meridian in autumn and disperses it in summer. In all seasons, it can treat the following disorders:
Pale, sticky stools (+).
Dark stools (-).
To encourage relaxation (-).
Pain in the groin (-), combined with point 6Sp (-).
Painful foot and big toe (-).
Insomnia (-).
Unpleasant smelling sweat (-).

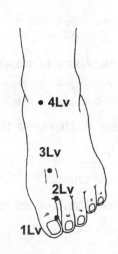

4Lv: Located in front of the ankle, on the same line as points 1Lv, 2Lv and 3Lv, between the two tendons.
This point boosts the Liver meridian in winter and disperses it at the end of summer. In all seasons, it can treat the following disorders:
Shivering (+).
Painful lower abdomen (-).
Seminal discharge in men (+).

5Lv: *Lo point*
Master point governing itching
Located in a small hollow on the inner side of the tibia, 5 fingerbreadths above the medial malleolus.
Itching (+), combined with point 30GB (-).
Pain or burning sensation in a phantom member (+, on the opposite side).

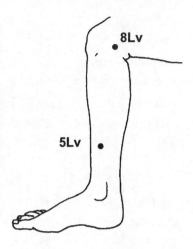

8Lv: Located on the inside of the crease formed when the knee is bent, touching the joint.
This point boosts the Liver meridian in its season – spring – and disperses it in autumn. In all seasons, it can treat the following disorders:
Hay fever (+).
Allergies (+).
Insufficient erections (+).
Premature ejaculation (+).
Vaginal itching (+).
Tendency to bruise easily (+).
Lack of assertiveness (+).

13Lv: *Mo point of the Spleen and the Pancreas*
Located at the tip of the eleventh rib.
Note: Stimulate this point only once you have boosted point 6CV.
As a tonic (+).
Craving for hot drinks (+).
Weariness (+).
Melancholy (+).
A feeling of cold throughout the body (+).
Parasites (+).

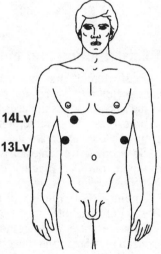

14F: *Mo point of the Liver*
Located between the sixth and seventh ribs, directly below the nipple.
Lazy liver (+).
Sleepiness after meals (+).
Blurred eyesight (+).
Difficulty in digesting (+).
Nausea (-).
Hangover (-), combined with points 3Lv (-) and 40GB (-).
Hot flushes during the menopause (+).
Discoloured and foul-smelling stools (+).
Lack of assertiveness (+).

Booster points

PM	L	LI	S	Sp	H	SI	B	K	MH	TH	GB	Lv
Spring	5	2	44	9	3	2	66	10	3	2	43	8
Summer	11	3	43	1	9	3	65	1	9	3	41	1
End Sum	10	5	41	2	8	5	60	2	8	6	38	2
Autumn	9	11	36	3	7	8	54	3	7	10	34	3
Winter	8	1	45	5	4	1	67	7	5	1	44	4

Dispersion points

PM	L	LI	S	Sp	H	SI	B	K	MH	TH	GB	Lv
Spring	10	5	41	2	8	5	60	2	8	6	38	2
Summer	9	11	36	3	7	8	54	3	7	10	34	3
End Sum	8	1	45	5	4	1	67	7	5	1	44	4
Autumn	5	2	44	9	3	2	66	10	3	2	43	8
Winter	11	3	43	1	9	3	65	1	9	3	41	1

Redistributing and balancing energy

Redistributing and balancing an individual's energy means harmonising the energy flowing through the person's meridians by using control points, known as the Booster points in the case of insufficiency or Dispersion points in the event of an excess. The Source point can also be used, either to replace one of these points or to complement it.

Sometimes, we come across an imbalance in one or more meridian pairs. For example, the Gall-Bladder PM could have an excess and the Liver PM, an insufficiency. This is when we should use the Lo point on the Gall-Bladder PM (ie, point 37GB) which will transfer the excess energy from the Gall-Bladder PM to the Liver PM.

However, it is quite common to find several Principal Meridians suffering from an imbalance and this is when we use the Extraordinary Vessels technique. This will allow us to obtain results in treating several disorders using few points since we only use the Key point on the Extraordinary Vessel, with its partner point, then its Entry point before rounding off with its Exit point.

Let's take the example of someone suffering from backache along each side of the spine, in other words along the course of the Bladder PM. This person will be nervous and will externalise a lot. They will have trouble sleeping and will complain of urinary disorders. This individual will derive great benefit from energy redistribution and balancing using the Yang Keo EV, in other words by dispersing Key point 62B, dispersing its partner point, 3SI, then dispersing its Exit point, 1B (see page 88).

CHAPTER 4

Extraordinary Vessels

Definition of Extraordinary Vessels

As well as the twelve Principal Meridians, we have at our disposal eight Extraordinary Vessels. These Vessels form a safety and regulation system governing the Principal Meridians.

Let's imagine that the Principal Meridians are rivers and in the event of heavy rain, we must open the lock gates to avoid the water rising and causing a flood.

Let's imagine that the Extraordinary Vessels are canals and that the Key point is the lock.

We could take the example of a subject suffering from an excess of yang energy in several yang Principal Meridians (Bladder, Gall-Bladder, Triple Heater, Large intestine, Small intestine and Stomach). This would result in jumpiness, insomnia, cramp, stiff muscles and especially backache (the back is very yang). These symptoms correspond to the Yang Keo Extraordinary Vessel.

All we have to do now is open the lock gate, ie, disperse the Key point on the Yang Keo Extraordinary Vessel, point 62B. We should combine this action with the stimulation of its partner point, 3SI, and to end, we stimulate its Exit point, 1B. See the corresponding points for each Extraordinary Vessel.

We shall soon realise that with these points alone, we have got rid of the backache, the jumpiness and the insomnia; and we now understand why these vessels are dubbed 'extraordinary'. They are also known as Exceptional Meridians or Curious Meridians – which is quite revealing!

These Extraordinary Vessels are therefore of great importance. They must be taken into account right from the start of a treatment if it is necessary to prepare the way. Once this has been achieved, the specific points of a 'recipe' can be added, if necessary.

Method of Treatment using Extraordinary Vessels

- Disperse the Key point;
- Disperse its partner point;
- Boost the Entry point;
- Disperse the Exit point of the Extraordinary Vessel.

Our choice of an Extraordinary Vessel will be guided by the symptoms presented or the energy balance.

Do not forget that a subject can present one or more of the symptoms listed. The same Extraordinary Vessel is therefore used for treating one or more symptoms.

Symptoms revealing an imbalance in the Extraordinary Vessels

Yang Keo
Excess yang
Stiffness and cramp in the back and spine
Jumpiness, insomnia, obsessional behaviour
Nervous tension
Exaggerated externalisation
Cramp, stiff muscles
Torticollis
Neuralgia, migraine, sciatica
Acne, boils

Yin Keo
Excess yin
Drowsiness
Frigidity
Premenstrual tension
Enuresia
Numbness, swelling
Prostate disorders, cystitis, urethritis

Yang Oe
The yang is calling for help
Pain in the shoulder muscles
Fever, shivering
Allergic reactions
Neuralgia, rheumatic pain
Recently developed buzzing in the ears
Sudden deafness, earache.

Yin Oe
The yin is asking for help
Pain in the region of the heart
A tight feeling in the chest (solar plexus),
anxiety, worry
Exaggerated emotional reactions
Psychopathy
Inflammation of the arteries
Spasms
Yin insomnia
Perturbed sexuality

Tae Mo
Obstruction between the upper and lower body
Venous circulation disorders (stasis of the vein
or lymphatic networks)
Flatulence
Back pain around the lumbar region
Pain on the outer side of the knee and the leg
Liver or gall-bladder disorders
Trembling

Tchrong Mo	Metabolic disorders (obesity, cellulite) Hormone disorders (overactive or underactive thyroid gland) Digestive disorders (wind) Gynaecological disorders (ovaries, uterus) Menstrual disorders Lumbago Spleen, liver, kidney disorders Pain on the inner side of the knee Groin pain
Conception	Yin PM overload Respiratory infections Sterility To assist birth Pain in the navel or on the sternum
Governing	General yang overload Torticollis, stiff back Stiffness in the arm and neck Pain in the spine Intercostal neuralgia Shingles Cervical arthritis Pain along the course of the Governing Vessel General weariness.

Yang Keo EV

Polarity:	Yang.
Description:	This vessel allows us to balance the yang meridians (Bladder, Gall-Bladder, Triple Heater, Large intestine, Small intestine, Stomach).
Symptoms:	Backache (particularly along the course of the Bladder PM, ie, down the spine). Yang insomnia. Exterior nervousness. Acne on the back. Cramp. Sciatica.
Treatment:	Disperse points 62B, 3SI and 1B.
Key point:	62B
Partner point:	3SI
Entry point:	62B
Exit point:	1B

Position of points

62B: Located in a small hollow 1 fingerbreadth below the lateral malleolus.

3SI: Located on the outer edge of the hand, in a small hollow touching the bony protuberance of the metacarpal/phalanx joint, in other words, at the end of the crease formed when the palm of the hand is curled up.

1B: Located at the inner corner of the eye.

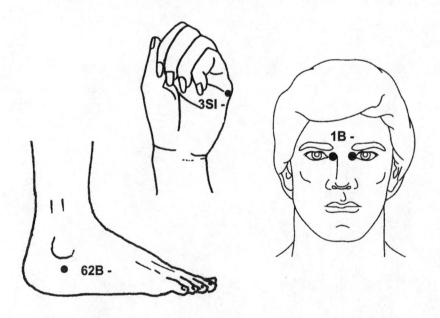

Disorders connected with the Yang Keo EV

Backache on either side of the spine (ie, along the Bladder PM)

Once you have stimulated the points along the Yang Keo EV, ie, points 62B-, 3SI- and 1B-, add the following points, if necessary:

54B-, 60B- and 67B- and round off the session by dispersing the painful points of the back, if required.

54B: Located right in the middle of the back of the knee.

60B: Located behind the lateral malleolus.

67B: Located at the outer corner of the small toenail.

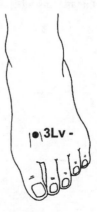

54B -

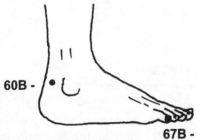

60B -

67B -

Insomnia in nervous subjects

Once you have stimulated the Yang Keo EV points, ie, points 62B-, 3SI- and 1B-, add the following points if necessary:

9L+ (if the subject is pale) or 9L- (if the subject has a high colour), 3Lv-, 14Lv-, 40GB- and 10TH-.

9L: Located in the groove of the radius, on the wrist crease, ie, before the radial styloid.

3Lv: Located at the tip of the angle formed by the first two metatarsals, visible when the toes are spread.

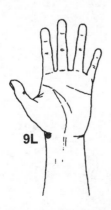

9L

3Lv -

14Lv: Located between the sixth and seventh ribs, directly below the nipple.

40GB: Located on the upper side of the foot, in a hollow in front of the lateral malleolus.

10TH: Located above the tip of the olecranon, in the hollow behind the elbow.

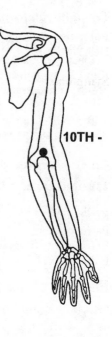

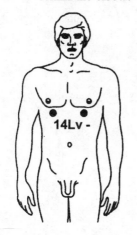

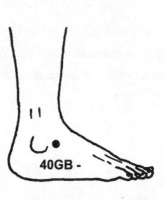

Nervousness – Agitation

Once you have stimulated the Yang Keo EV points, ie, points 62B-, 3SI- and 1B-, add the following points if necessary:

36S-, 4LI- and 3Lv-.

36S: Located 4 fingerbreadths below the knee, in the hollow between the muscles.

4LI: Located in the angle formed by the first two metacarpals, touching the base of the second metacarpal.

3Lv: Located at the tip of the angle formed by the first two metatarsals when the toes are spread.

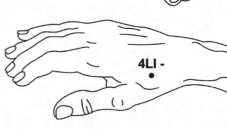

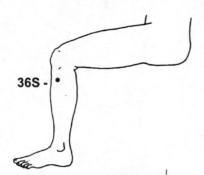

Yin Keo EV

Polarity:	Yin.
Description:	This vessel is perfect for treating disorders due to yin imbalances.
Symptoms:	Drowsiness.
	Premenstrual tension.
	Tender breasts before periods.
	Genital and urinary problems (metritis, nephritis, inflammation of the ovaries, cystitis, urine retention, prostatitis, urethritis, vaginal discharge).
Treatment:	Disperse points 6K, 7L and 1B.

Key point:	6K
Partner point:	7L
Entry point:	6K
Exit point:	1B

Position of points

6K: Located 1 fingerbreadth below the medial malleolus.

7L: Located on the forearm, 3 fingerbreadths above the wrist crease, in the groove of the radius where one can feel the pulse.

1B: Located at the inner corner of the eye.

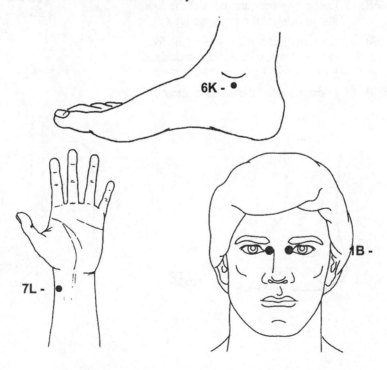

91

Disorders connected with the Yin Keo EV

Cystitis – Urethritis

Once you have stimulated the Yin Keo EV points, ie, points 6K-, 7L- and 1B-, add the following points if necessary:

2CV-, 3CV-, 4CV-, 27B-, 28B-, 65B-, 64B- and 60B-.

Recommended essential oil: Karnataka sandalwood (rubbed into the lower abdomen).

2CV: Located on the median line of the lower abdomen, above the pubis.

3CV: Located on the median line of the lower abdomen, 1 fingerbreadth above the pubis.

4CV: Located 1 thumb's breadth above point 3CV.

27B: Located 2 fingerbreadths outside the first sacral hollow.

28B: Located 2 fingerbreadths outside the second sacral hollow.

65B: Located on the outer edge of the foot, just in front of the small toe joint.

64B: Located on the outer edge of the foot, just in front of the fifth metatarsal joint.

60B: Located behind the lateral malleolus.

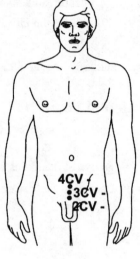

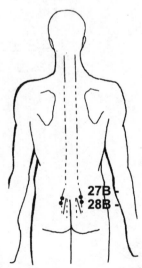

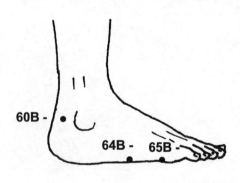

Prostatitis

Once you have stimulated the Yin Keo EV points, ie, points 6K-, 7L- and 1B-, add the following points if necessary:

54B-, 2CV-, 3CV-, 4CV-, 67B+, 64B+ and 28B+.

54B: Located right in the centre of the back of the knee.

2CV: Located on the median line of the lower abdomen, above the pubis.

3CV: Located on the median line of the lower abdomen, 1 fingerbreadth above the pubis.

4CV: Located 1 thumb's breadth above point 3CV.

67B: Located at the outer corner of the small toenail.

64B: Located on the outside edge of the foot, in front of the fifth metatarsal joint.

28B: Located 2 fingerbreadths outside the second sacral hollow.

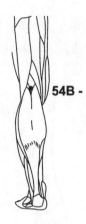

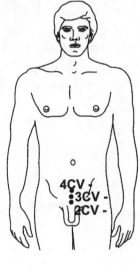

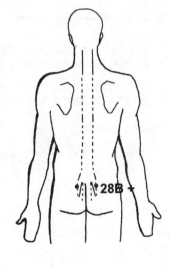

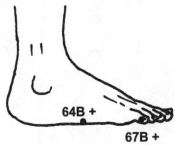

Premenstrual tension

Once you have stimulated the Yin Keo EV points, ie, points 6K-, 7L- and 1B-, add the following points if necessary:

60B-, 3CV-, 6Sp- and 10Sp-.

60B: Located behind the lateral malleolus.

3CV: Located on the median line of the lower abdomen, 1 fingerbreadth above the pubis.

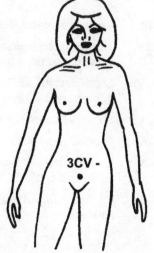

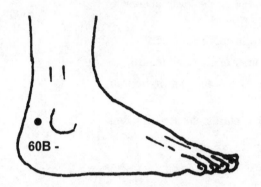

6Sp: Located on the inside of the leg, 4 fingerbreadths above the medial malleolus, in a hollow behind the tibia.

10Sp: Located on the upper side of the thigh, slightly to the inside, in a hollow 4 fingerbreadths above the knee.

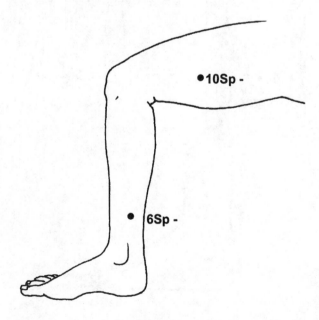

94

Drowsiness

Once you have stimulated the Yin Keo EV points, ie, points 6K-, 7L- and 1B-, add the following points if necessary:

62B+, 4LI+, 36S+ and 12CV+.

62B: Located below the lateral malleolus.

4LI: Located in the angle formed by the first two metacarpals, in front of and at the base of the second metacarpal.

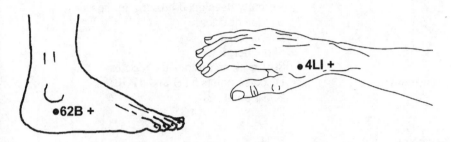

36S: Located 4 fingerbreadths below the knee, between the peroneous longus and the extensor digitorum communis longus.

12CV: Located halfway between the navel and the xiphisternum.

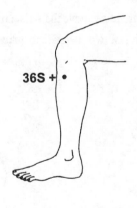
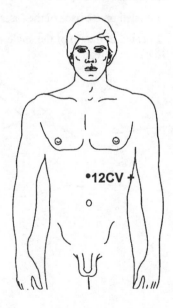

Yang Oe EV

Polarity:	Yang.
Description:	The yang is calling for help.
	The yang corresponds to the outside
	and everything that allows us to link
	up with things connected with the
	outside (joints, ears and skin).
Symptoms:	Joint pain, in particular in the wrist
	(due to atmospheric changes).
	Earache.
	Recently developed buzzing in the ears.
	Sudden deafness.
	Dermatosis.
	Skin allergies.
	Stiff neck and trapezius muscles.
Treatment:	Disperse points 5TH and 41GB;
	Boost point 63B;
	Disperse point 14GV.
Key point:	5TH
Partner point:	41GB
Entry point:	63B
Exit point:	14GV

Position of points

5TH: Located on the back of the forearm, 2 fingerbreadths above the wrist crease.

41GB: Located at the tip of the angle formed by the last two metatarsals when the toes are spread.

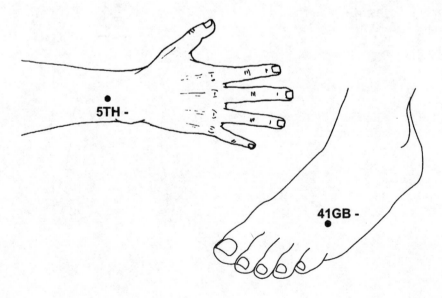

63B: Located 3 fingerbreadths in front of and below the lateral maelleolus, in a hollow.

14GV: Located on the back, between the cervical and the dorsal vertebrae.

Note: To differentiate between the cervical and the dorsal vertebrae, turn the subject's head to one side; the cervical vertebrae rotate, unlike the dorsal vertebrae which are held in position by the ribs. Point 14GV is therefore in between the cervical vertebrae which pivot and the dorsal vertebrae which hardly move at all. Moreover, there is often a 'bison's hump' at this spot, which is a helpful guide.

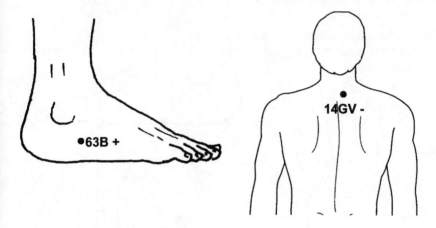

Disorders connected with the Yang Oe EV

Earache

Once you have stimulated the Yang Oe EV points, ie, points 5TH-, 41GB-, 63B+ and 14GV-, add the following points if necessary:

17TH-, 18TH-, 19TH- and 20TH-

Recommended essential oil: Eucalyptus (rubbed around the ear).

17TH: All located in the small hollows
18TH: surrounding the rear of the ear.
19TH:
20TH:

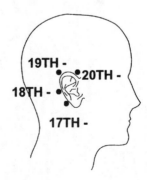

Buzzing in the ears

Once you have stimulated the Yang Oe EV points, ie, points 5TH-, 41GB-, 63B+ and 14GV-, add the following points if necessary:

62B-, 7MH- (in the case of high blood pressure), 9MH+ (in the case of low blood pressure), 15B-, 23B+, 17SI-, 5SI- and 6SI-.

62B: Located below the lateral malleolus.

7MH: Located in the centre of the inner wrist crease.

9MH: Located at the corner of the middle fingernail, alongside the index finger.

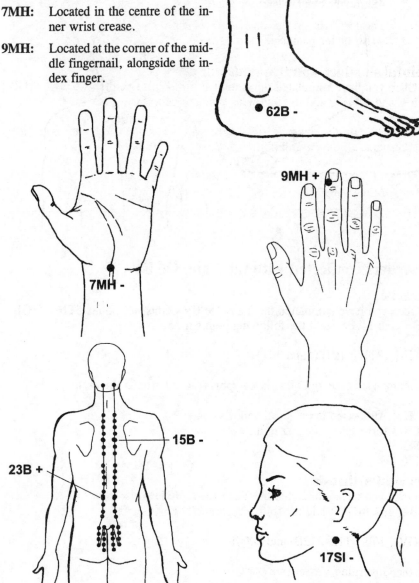

15B: Located level with the fifth and sixth dorsal vertebrae.

23B: Located level with the second and third lumbar vertebrae.

17SI: Located on the side of the neck, behind the lower angle of the jaw, in front of the sternocleidomastoid muscle.

5SI: Located in the hollow just below point 4SI, on the other side of the joint.

6SI: Located right on the outer edge of the wrist, on the palm side.

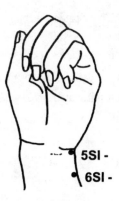

Painful shoulder and trapezius muscle
Once you have stimulated the Yang Oe EV points, ie, points 5TH-, 41GB-, 63B+ and 14GV-, add the following points if necessary:

Point 37S+, on the opposite side to the pain and point 1TH+ on both sides, then disperse all the painful points in the shoulder region.

37S: Located slightly above the middle of the lower leg, four fingerbreadths below point 36S.

1TH: Located at the corner of the fourth fingernail, alongside the little finger.

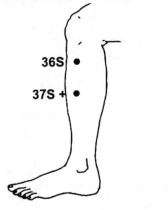
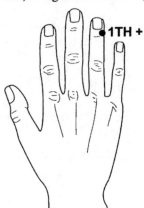

Cervical arthrosis
Once you have stimulated the Yang Oe EV points, ie, points 5TH-, 41GB-, 63B+ and 14GV-, add the following points if necessary:

16GV-, 10B-, 11B-, 12B- and 20GB-.

Or the Governing Vessel (see page 141).

16GV: Located on the rear median line of the body, at the nape of the neck, just below the occiput (the back of the skull).

10B: Located at the back of the neck, below the occipital protuberances.

11B: Located level with the first dorsal vertebra.

12B: Located level with the second and third dorsal vertebrae.

20GB: Located at the back of the neck, below the occipital protuberances.

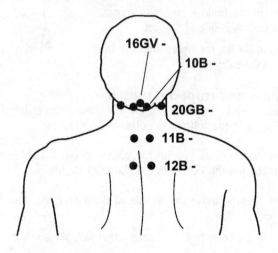

Pain at the back of the wrist

Once you have stimulated the Yang Oe EV points, ie, points 5TH-, 41GB-, 63B+ and 14GV-, add the following points if necessary:

1TH+ and 4TH-.

1TH: Located at the outer corner of the fourth fingernail, alongside the little finger.

4TH: Located on the crease on the back of the wrist.

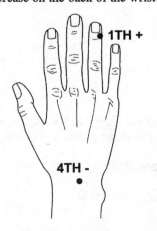

Yin Oe EV

Polarity:	Yin.
Description:	The yin is calling for help.
	The yin corresponds to the inside, our
	feelings, the heart, sexuality and rest.
	Such subjects are upset when things
	do not go according to plan.
Symptoms:	Internalisation.
	Nervous pain in the region of the heart.
	Yin insomnia.
	Loss of word memory.
	Sexual disorders.
	Spasms.
Treatment:	Disperse points 6MH and 4Sp;
	Boost point 9K;
	Disperse point 23CV.
Key point:	6MH
Partner point:	4Sp
Entry point:	9K
Exit point:	23CV

Position of points

6MH: Located on the front of the forearm, 3 fingerbreadths above the wrist crease, between the two tendons.

4Sp: Located halfway up the inside edge of the foot, ie, where the dorsal skin and the sole of the foot meet.

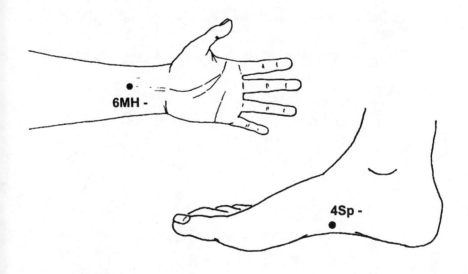

9K: Located on the inside of the leg, 7 fingerbreadths above the medial malleolus, below the mass of the calf muscle, in a hollow slightly behind the tibia.

23CV: Located exactly on the median line above the 'Adam's apple'.

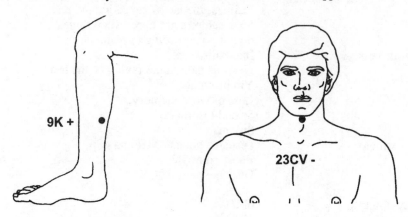

Disorders connected with the Yin Oe EV

Pain in the region of the heart

Once you have stimulated the Yin Oe EV points, ie, points 6MH-, 4Sp-, 9K+ and 23CV-, add the following points if necessary:

21Sp-, 9MH+, 1SP+, 3K- and 3Lv-.

Recommended plant: Angelica

21Sp: Located on the side of the thorax, in the sixth intercostal space, ie, in the centre.

9MH: Located at the corner of the middle fingernail, alongside the index finger.

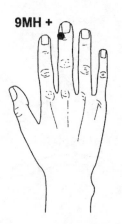

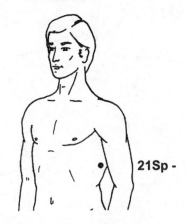

1Sp: Located at the outer corner of the big toenail.

3K: Located just behind the medial malleolus.

3Lv: Located at the tip of the angle formed by the first two metatarsals when the toes are spread.

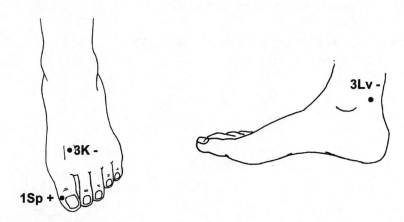

Failing memory

Once you have stimulated the Yin Oe EV points, ie, points 6MH-, 4Sp-, 9K+ and 23CV-, add the following points if necessary:

19GV+, 20GV+, 2Sp+, 41S+, 3H+, 3SI+ and 9MH+.

19GV: Located on the top of the head, level with the join between the parietal and occipital bones.

20GV: Located on the top of the head, on a line drawn between the tops of the ears.

2Sp: Located on the inside of the foot, just in front of the big toe joint.

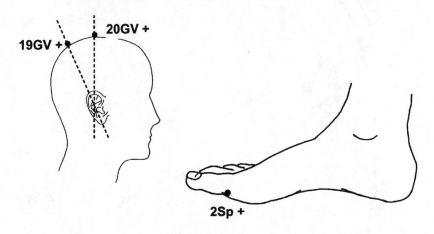

41S: Located right in the centre of the front of the ankle, in between the tendons.

3H: Located on the inside crease formed when the elbow is bent, level with the joint.

3SI: Located just after the metacarpal/phalanx joint.

9MH: Located at the inner corner of the middle fingernail.

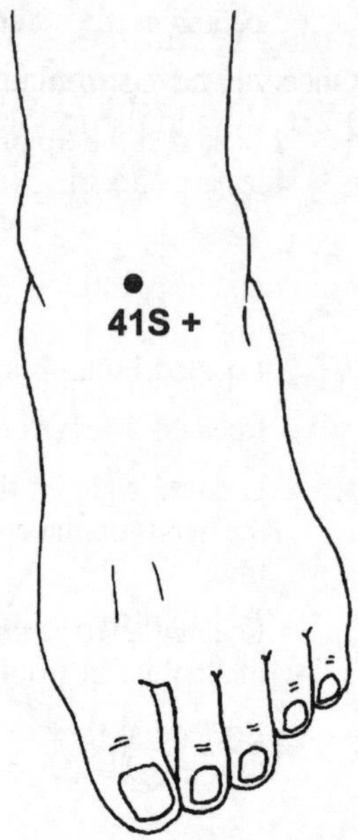

41S +

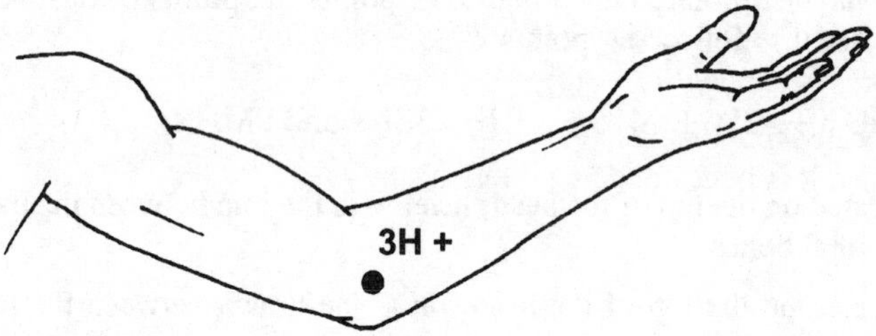

3H +

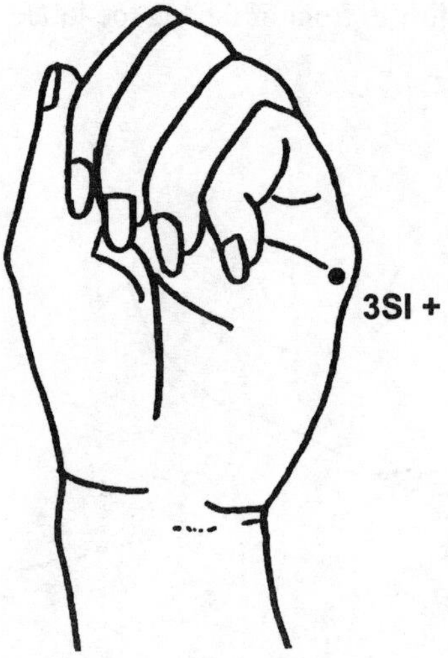

3SI +

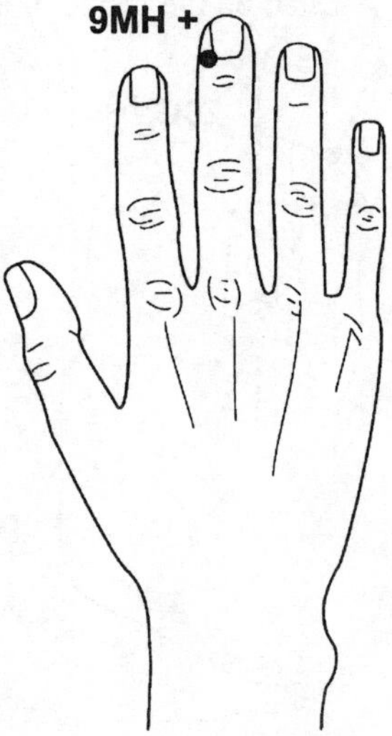

9MH +

Waning sexuality

Once you have stimulated the Yin Oe EV points, ie, points 6MH-, 4Sp-, 9K+ and 23CV-, add the following points if necessary:

5CV+, 6CV+, 8MH+, 7K+, 10K+, 23B+, 4GV+ and 8Lv+.

Recommended plant: Ginseng

5CV: Located 1 thumb's breadth above point 4CV.

6CV: Located 2 fingerbreadths below the navel.

8MH: Located right in the middle of the palm of the hand, on the crease that crosses the heart line.

7K: Located 2 fingerbreadths above the medial malleolus, in front of the Achilles' tendon.

10K: Located in the crease formed when the knee is bent.

23B: Located level with the second and third lumbar vertebrae.

4GV: Located in the hollow of the back, between the second and third lumbar vertebrae.

8Lv: Located on the inside crease of the knee when it is bent, touching the joint.

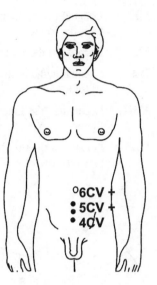

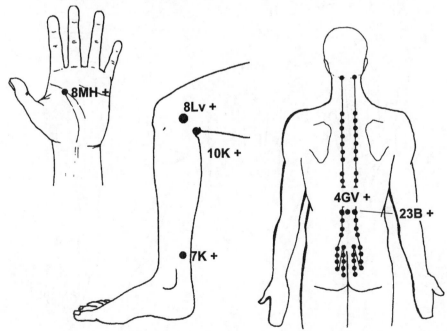

Slow microcirculation (Raynaud's disease)

Once you have stimulated the Yin Oe EV points, ie, points 6MH-, 4Sp-, 9K+ and 23CV-, add the following points if necessary:

3H-, 32S-, 9L+, 9MH+ and 3Lv-.

Recommended plant: Gingko biloba

3H: Located on the inside of the crease formed when the elbow is bent, level with the joint.

32S: Located in the middle of the front of the thigh.

9L: Located in the groove of the radius, on the wrist crease, ie, above the radial styloid.

9MH: Located at the inner corner of the middle fingernail, alongside the index finger.

3Lv: Located at the tip of the angle formed by the first two metatarsals when the toes are spread.

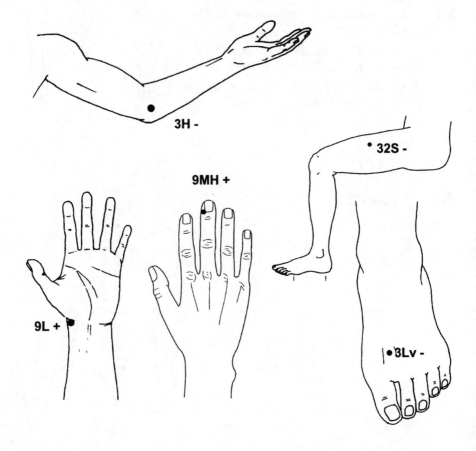

Spasms in the lower abdomen as a result of anger

Once you have stimulated the Yin Oe EV points, ie, points 6MH-, 4Sp-, 9K+ and 23CV-, add the following points if necessary:

9Sp-, 36S- and 3Lv-.

9Sp: Located just below the inside of the knee, touching the tibia joint.

36S: Located 4 fingerbreadths below the knee, between the peroneous longus and the extensor digitorum communis longus.

3Lv: Located at the tip of the angle formed by the first two metatarsals when the toes are spread.

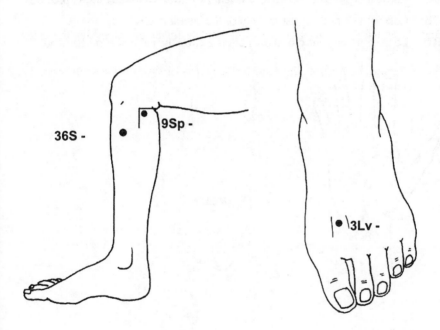

Yin insomnia in introverts who bottle up their feelings

Once you have stimulated the Yin Oe EV points, ie, points 6MH-, 4Sp-, 9K+ and 23CV-, add the following points if necessary:

9L- (if the subject is pale) or 9L+ (if the subject is highly coloured), 3Lv-, 14Lv-, 40GB- and 7MH-.

9L: Located in the radial groove, on the wrist crease, ie, before the radial styloid.

3Lv: Located at the tip of the angle formed by the first two metatarsals when the toes are spread.

14Lv: Located between the sixth and seventh ribs, directly below the nipple.

40GB: Located in a hollow just in front of the lateral malleolus.

7MH: Located in the centre of the wrist crease, on the palm side of the hand.

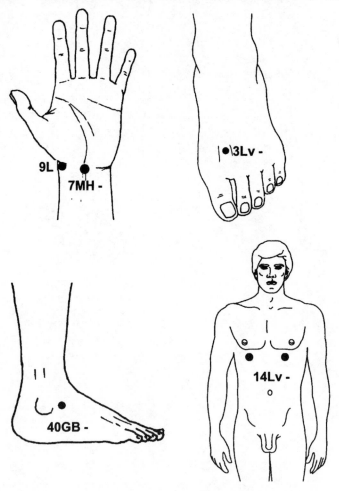

Tae Mo EV

Polarity:
Yang.

Description:
This Extraordinary Vessel is the one most often stimulated since it is connected with the gall-bladder and the liver. It is a belt-shaped Extraordinary Vessel and any obstruction can cause an imbalance between the upper and the lower halves of the body. The result is often poor circulation in the legs, which encourages cellulite, particularly around the upper thighs.

Occasional cases of paralysis of the legs have been known, resulting from the obstruction of this Extraordinary Vessel. The author himself has freed six such pseudo-paralyses in just a few minutes, including one on an Alsatian dog.

Symptoms:
Lumbago around the back.
Tired and heavy legs.
Hip pain.
Certain pains in the knee, the outer leg and the shoulder.
Gynaecological disorders.
Wind.
Constipation.
Pins and needles in the legs.

Treatment:
Disperse points 41GB and 5TH;
Boost point 26GB;
Disperse points 27GB and 27GB.

Key point:	41GB
Partner point:	5TH
Entry point:	26GB
Point of passage:	27GB
Exit point:	28GB

Position of points

41GB: Located at the tip of the angle formed by the last two metatarsals when the toes are spread.

5TH: Located on the back of the forearm, 2 fingerbreadths above the wrist crease.

26GB: Located on the sides of the abdomen, level with the navel, between the bottom of the ribcage and the ridge of the pelvis.

27GB: Located above the upper edge of the front of the hip bone.

28GB: Located below the hip bone.

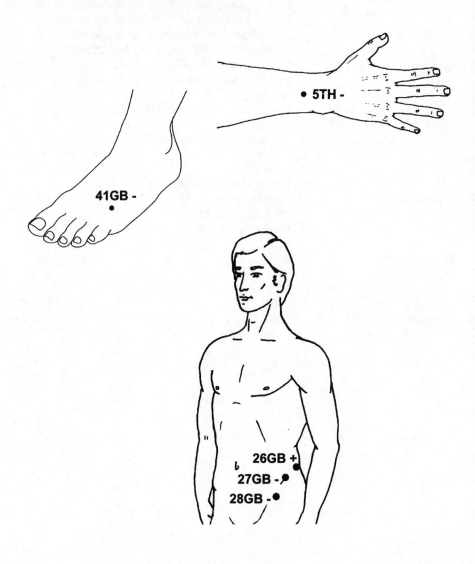

Disorders connected with the Tae Mo EV

Back pain spreading round the back

Once you have stimulated the Tae Mo EV points, ie, points 41GB-, 5TH-, 26GB+, 27GB- and 28GB-, add the following points if necessary:

54B-, 60B-, 67B-.

54B: Located right in the centre of the back of the knee.

60B: Located behind the lateral malleolus.

67B: Located at the outer corner of the small toenail.

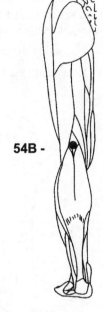

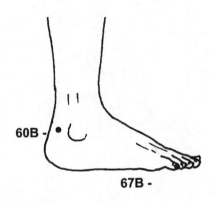

Hip pain

Once you have stimulated the Tae Mo EV points, ie, points 41GB-, 5TH-, 26GB+, 27GB- and 28GB-, add the following points if necessary:

On the painless side: 44GB+, 43GB+, 1Lv+ and 8Lv+;
On the painful side: 5Lv-, 30GB-, 1GB-; then point 20GV-.

44GB: Located at the outer corner of the fourth toenail.

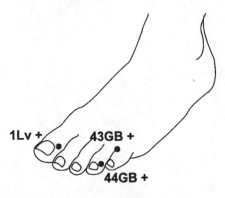

43GB: Located in between the fourth and small toes.

1Lv: Located on the inner corner of the big toenail.

8Lv: Located on the inside of the crease formed when the knee is bent, touching the joint.

5Lv: Located in a small hollow on the inside of the tibia, 5 fingerbreadths above the medial malleolus.

30GB: Located behind the greater trochanter, the bony protuberance one can feel in the buttock, especially when the leg is rotated.

1GB: Located at the outer corner of the eye.

20GV: Located on the top of the head, on a line joining the tops of the ears.

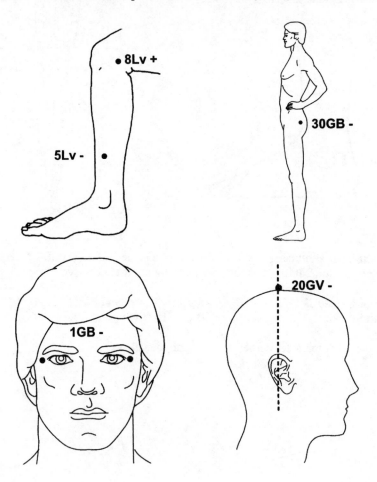

Pain in both hips

Once you have stimulated the Tae Mo EV points, ie, points 41GB-, 5TH-, 26GB+, 27GB- and 28GB-, add the following points if necessary:

30GB-, 54B-, 60B- and 8K-.

30GB: Located behind the trochanter, the bony bump one can feel in the buttock, especially when the leg is rotated.

54B: Located right in the centre of the back of the knee.

60B: Located behind the lateral malleolus.

8K: Located in front of point 7K, on the edge of the tibia.

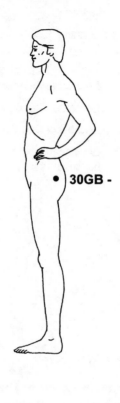

30GB -

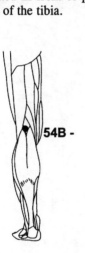

54B -

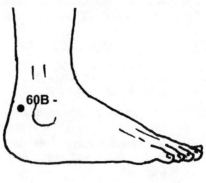

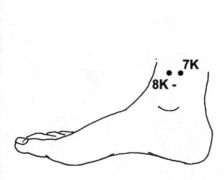

Pain or swelling on the outside of the knees

Once you have stimulated the Tae Mo EV points, ie, points 41GB-, 5TH-, 26GB+, 27GB- and 28GB-, add the following points if necessary:

45S+, 1Sp+, 1Lv+, 44GB+, 34GB+, then disperse all the painful points around the knee.

45S: Located at the outer corner of the second toenail.

1Sp: Located at the inner corner of the big toenail.

1Lv: Located at the inner corner of the big toenail.

44GB: Located at the outer corner of the fourth toenail.

34GB: Located just below the outer side of the knee, below the head of the fibula, the small bony protuberance one can feel just below the back of the knee.

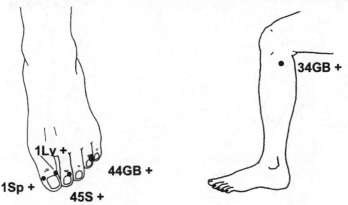

Poor circulation in the legs

Once you have stimulated the Tae Mo EV points, ie, points 41GB-, 5TH-, 26GB+, 27GB- and 28GB-, add the following points if necessary:

32S-, 36S-, 5Sp-, 6Sp-, 10Sp-, 1Lv+, 2Lv- and 3Lv-.

32S: Located in the centre of the front of the thigh.

36S: Located 4 fingerbreadths below the knee, between the peroneous longus and the extensor digitorum cummunis longus.

5Sp: Located in front of the medial malleolus, on the front of the foot, inside the tendon of the peroneous longus in the hollow formed when the foot is turned inwards.

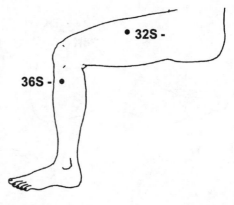

6Sp: Located on the inside of the leg, 4 fingerbreadths above the medial malleolus, in a hollow behind the tibia.

10Sp: Located on the upper side of the thigh, slightly to the inside, in a hollow 4 fingerbreadths above the knee.

1Lv: Located at the inner corner of the big toenail.

2Lv: Located between the first two toes.

3Lv: Located at the tip of the angle formed by the first two metatarsals when the toes are spread.

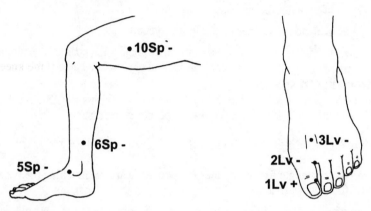

Wind

Once you have stimulated the Tae Mo EV points, ie, points 41GB-, 5TH-, 26GB+, 27GB- and 28GB-, add the following points if necessary:

5Sp+, 3LI- and 36S+.

5Sp: Located in front of the medial malleolus, on the front of the foot, inside the tendon of the peroneous longus in the hollow formed when the foot is turned inwards.

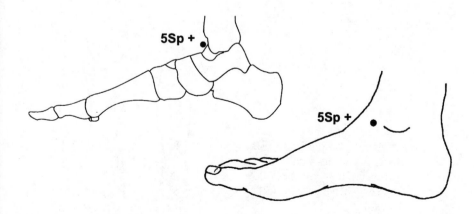

3LI: Located just after the metacarpal/phalanx joint, on the inside.

36S: Located 4 fingerbreadths below the knee, between the peroneous longus and the extensor digitorum communis longus.

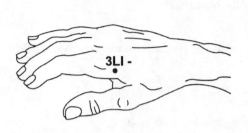

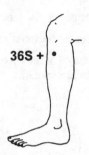

Constipation due to spasms

Once you have stimulated the Tae Mo EV points, ie, points 41GB-, 5TH-, 26GB+, 27GB- and 28GB-, add the following points if necessary:

4LI-, 2LI- (except in spring), 25S- and 6TH-.

4LI: Located in the angle formed by the first two metacarpals, touching the base of the first metacarpal.

2LI: Located just in front of the metacarpal/phalanx joint, on the inside edge of the index finger.

25S: Located 3 fingerbreadths outside the navel.

6TH: Located 3 fingerbreadths above the wrist crease on the back of the hand, between the two bones of the forearm.

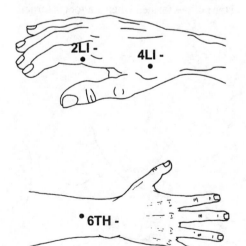

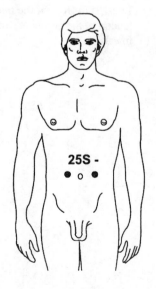

Tchrong Mo EV

Polarity: Yin.

Description: This Extraordinary Vessel can avoid many gynaecological problems such as menstrual disorders, cysts of the ovaries or the breasts, and fibromas. It can also help to regulate hormonal activities, especially those dependent on the thyroid.

It is connected with the Sp, Lv and K EVs.

Symptoms: Absence of menstruation.
Nausea with pain in the region of the heart.
Underactive thyroid gland.
Overactive thyroid gland.
Wind, flatulence.
Bloated feeling in stomach.
Congestion in the lower abdomen.
Constipation or diarrhoea.
Groin pain (can avoid hernias and prolapses).
Pain on the inside of the knee and the big toe.
Digestive disorders.
Bedwetting.
Sterility.
Gynaecological problems.
Hysterectomy.

Treatment: Disperse points 4Sp and 6MH;
Boost point 11K;
Disperse point 21K.

Key point: 4Sp

Partner point: 6MH

Entry point: 11K

Exit point: 21K

Position of points

4Sp: Located halfway up the inside of the foot, on the line between the dorsal skin and the sole of the foot.

6MH: Located on the front of the forearm, 3 fingerbreadths above the wrist crease, between the two tendons.

11K: Located just above the pubis, on either side of the median line; the two points are 3 fingerbreadths apart.

21K: Located below the ribs; the two points are 3 fingerbreadths apart.

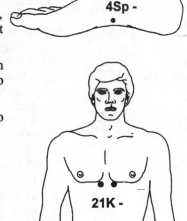

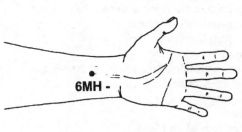

Disorders connected with the Tchrong Mo EV

Late or insufficient menstruation

Once you have stimulated the Tchrong Mo EV points, ie, points 4Sp-, 6MH-, 11K+ and 21K-, add the following points if necessary:

6Sp-, 10Sp-, 4LI+, 1Lv+, 8Lv+, 14Lv+ and 18B+.

6Sp: Located on the inside of the leg, 4 fingerbreadths above the medial malleolus, in a hollow behind the tibia.

10Sp: Located on the front of the thigh, slightly to the inside, in a hollow 4 fingerbreadths above the knee.

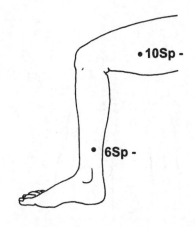

4LI: Located in the angle formed by the first two metacarpals, in front of and touching the base of the second metacarpal.

1Lv: Located at the outer corner of the big toenail.

8Lv: Located on the inside of the knee crease, touching the joint.

14Lv: Located between the sixth and seventh ribs, directly below the nipple.

18B: Located level with the ninth and tenth dorsal vertebrae.

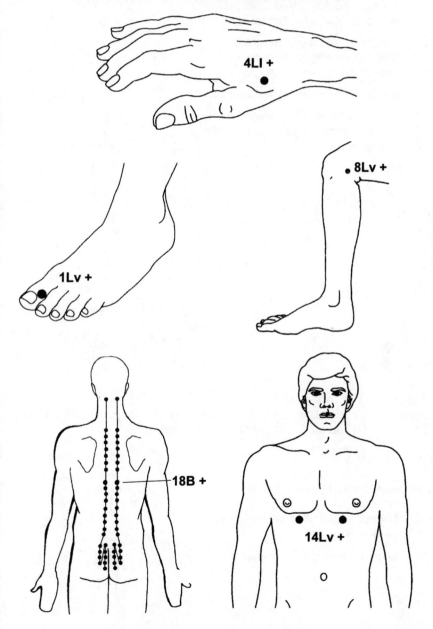

Heavy menstruation

Once you have stimulated the Tchrong Mo EV points, ie, points 4Sp-, 6MH-, 11K+ and 21K-, add the following points if necessary:

6Sp+, 4LI-, 2Lv- and 3Lv-.

6Sp: Located on the inside of the lower leg, 4 fingerbreadths above the medial malleolus, in a hollow behind the tibia.

4LI: Located in the angle formed by the first two metacarpals, touching the front of the second metacarpal.

2Lv: Located in between the first two toes.

3Lv: Located at the tip of the angle formed by the first two metatarsals, when the toes are spread.

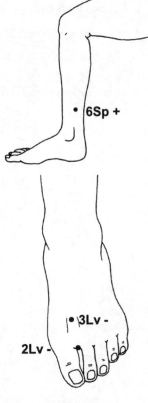

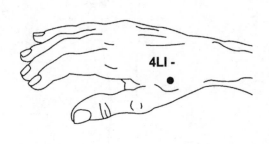

Underactive thyroid gland

Once you have stimulated the Tchrong Mo EV points, ie, points 4Sp-, 6MH-, 11K+ and 21K-, add the following points if necessary:

22CV+ and 23CV+.

Recommended trace element: Iodine.

22CV: Located in the hollow above the fork of the sternum.

23CV: Located above the Adam's apple.

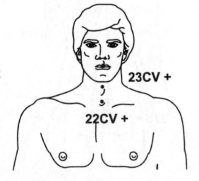

Painful lower abdomen

Once you have stimulated the Tchrong Mo EV points, ie, points 4Sp-, 6MH-, 11K+ and 21K-, add the following points if necessary:

9Sp-, 1Lv+, 2Lv+ and 3Lv+.

9Sp: Located just below the inside of the knee, touching the bony protuberance of the tibia.

1Lv: Located at the outer corner of the big toenail.

2Lv: Located in between the first two toes.

3Lv: Located at the tip of the angle formed by the first two metatarsals when the toes are spread.

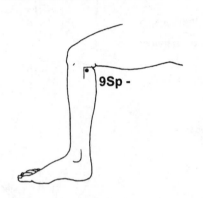

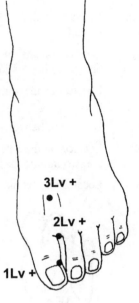

Diarrhoea

Once you have stimulated the Tchrong Mo EV points, ie, points 4Sp-, 6MH-, 11K+ and 21K-, add the following points if necessary:

37S+, 4LI+ and 25S+.

37S: Located slightly above the middle of the lower leg, 4 fingerbreadths below point 36S.

4LI: Located in the angle formed by the first two metacarpals, touching the front of the base of the second metacarpal.

25S: Located three fingerbreadths either side of the navel.

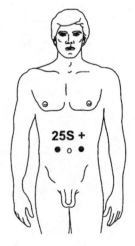

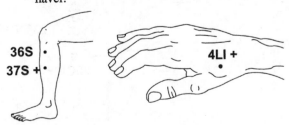

Pain on the inside of the knee

Once you have stimulated the Tchrong Mo EV points, ie, points 4Sp-, 6MH-, 11K+ and 21K-, add the following points if necessary:

1Sp+, 2Sp+, 1Lv+, 2Lv+, 1K+ and 3K+, and disperse the painful points around the knee.

1Sp: Located at the inner corner of the big toenail.

2Sp: Located on the inside of the foot, just below the big toe joint.

1Lv: Located at the outer corner of the big toenail.

2Lv: Located in between the first two toes.

1K: Located on the sole of the foot, between the two muscle masses.

3K: Located just behind the medial malleolus.

Conception EV

Polarity:	Yin.
Description:	This vessel is the sea of the yin PMs.
	As well as being an Extraordinary Vessel with a key opening point, the Conception Vessel - just like the Governing Vessel – has a series of its own points along its course.
	It is median, therefore unilateral.
Symptoms:	Conception problems (sterility).
	Respiratory infections (coughs, asthma, sinusitis, laryngitis, hay fever, sneezing).
	Burns.
	Sunburn.
	Allergies.
Treatment:	Disperse points 7L, 6K, 1CV and 24CV

Key point:	7L
Partner point:	6K
Entry point:	1CV
Exit point:	24CV

Position of points

7L: Located in a hollow 3 fingerbreadths above the wrist crease, just above the radial styloid.

6K: Located in a hollow just below the medial malleolus.

1CV: Located on the floor of the pelvis, between the anus and the genitalia.

24CV: Located in the hollow between the tip of the chin and the lower lip.

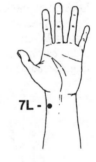

7L -

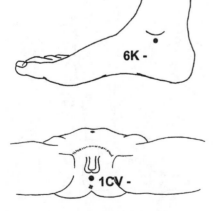

6K -

1CV -

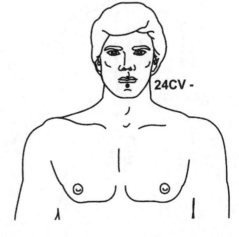

24CV -

Disorders connected with the Conception EV

Infertility

Stimulate the Conception EV and the Tchrong Mo EV points alternately once every fifteen days, ie, twice a month, leaving a gap of one week between the stimulation of the Conception and the Tchrong Mo EVs.

Specific points to add to the Conception EV, ie, points 7L-, 6K-, 1CV- and 24CV- (once a fortnight):

5CV+, 6CV+, 4GV+, 23B+, 9K+, 30S+ and 2CV+ (once a fortnight).

5CV: Located 1 thumb's breadth above point 4CV.

6CV: Located 2 fingerbreadths below the navel.

4GV: Located in the hollow on the back, level with the kidneys, between the second and third lumbar vertebrae.

23B: Located level with the second and third lumbar vertebrae.

9K: Located on the inside of the leg, 7 fingerbreadths above the medial malleolus, below the mass of the calf muscle, in a hollow 3 fingerbreadths behind the tibia.

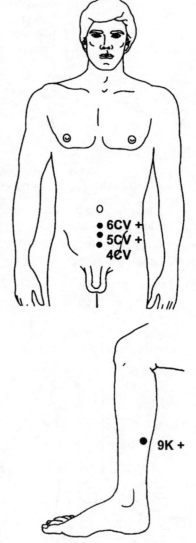

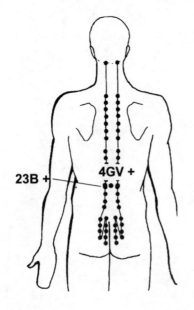

124

30S: Located above the pubis, 3 fingerbreadths outside the median line.

2CV: Located just above the pubis.

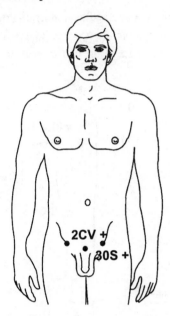

Infertility (Continued)

Stimulate the Conception EV and the Tchrong Mo EV points alternately once every fifteen days, ie, twice a month, leaving a gap of one week between the stimulation of the Conception and the Tchrong Mo EVs.

Specific points to add to the Tchrong Mo EV, ie, points 6MH-, 4Sp-, 11K+ and 21K- (once every 15 days, alternating with the specific points given on pages 118):

6Sp+, 1Lv+, 8Lv+, 14Lv+, 18B+ and 9K+.

6Sp: Located on the inside of the leg, 4 fingerbreadths above the medial malleolus, in a hollow behind the tibia.

1Lv: Located at the outer angle of the big toenail.

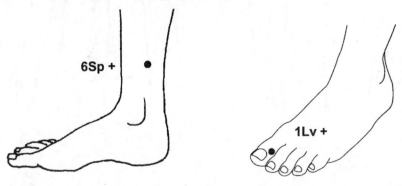

8Lv: Located on the inside of the knee crease, touching the joint.

14Lv: Located between the sixth and seventh ribs, directly below the nipple.

18B: Located level with the ninth and tenth dorsal vertebrae.

9K: Located on the inside of the leg, 7 fingerbreadths above the medial malleolus, below the mass of the calf muscle, in a hollow slightly behind the tibia.

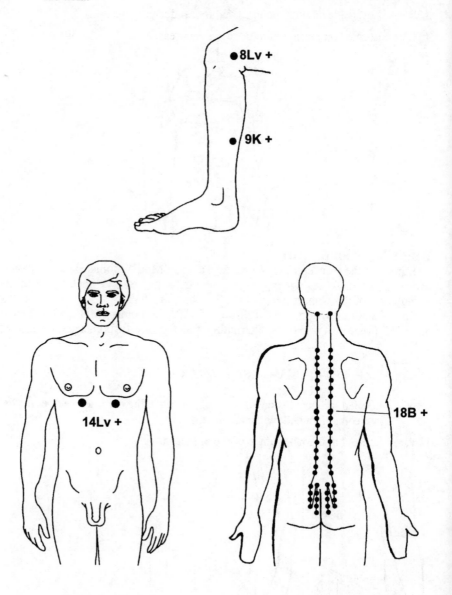

Coughs – Asthma

Once you have stimulated the Conception EV points, ie, points 7L-, 6K-, 1CV- and 24CV- , add the following points, if necessary:

22CV-, 13B- and 17CV+.

22CV: Located in the hollow above the fork of the sternum.

13B: Located level with the third and fourth dorsal vertebrae.

17CV: Located on the sternum, between the breasts.

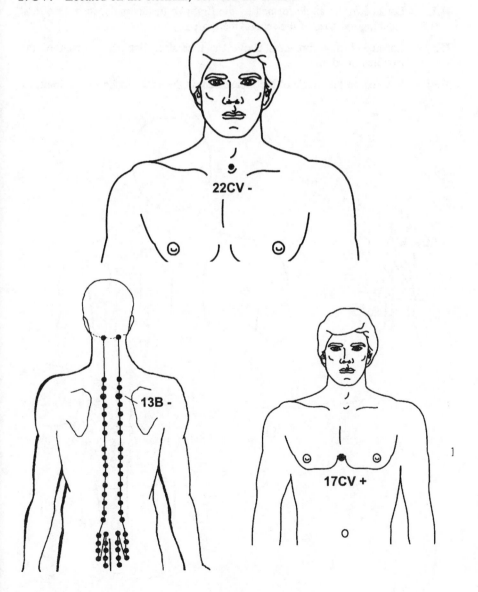

Allergies – Hay fever – Sneezing

Once you have stimulated the Conception EV points, ie, points 7L-, 6K-, 1CV- and 24CV- , add the following points, if necessary:

5L-, 12B-, 4LI-, 7K+ and 8Lv+.

5L: Located in the centre of the crease of the elbow, touching the tendon of the biceps.

12B: Located level with the second and third dorsal vertebrae.

4LI: Located in the angle formed by the first two metacarpals, in front of and touching the base of the second metacarpal.

7K: Located 2 fingerbreadths above the medial malleolus, in front of the Achilles' tendon.

8Lv: Located on the inside of the crease behind the knee, touching the joint.

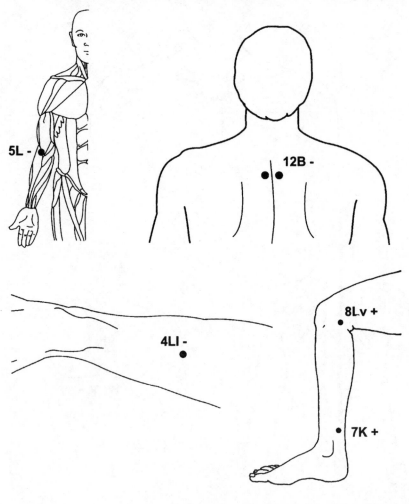

Burns – Sunburn

Once you have stimulated the Conception EV points, ie, points 7L-, 6K-, 1CV- and 24CV- , add the following points, if necessary:

39GB+, 6Sp+ and then disperse all the points surrounding the affected area.

39GB: Located 2 fingerbreadths above the medial malleolus, on the fibula.

6Sp: Located on the inside of the leg, 4 fingerbreadths above the medial malleolus, in a hollow behind the tibia.

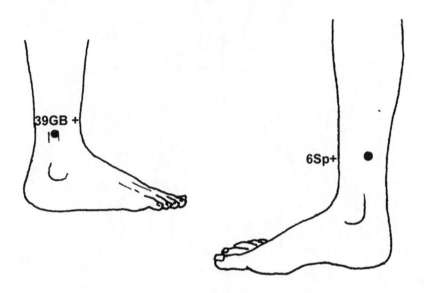

Conception Vessel

Polarity: Yin.

Course: The Conception Vessel starts between the anus and the genitalia, runs across the navel and the sternum as far as the chin.

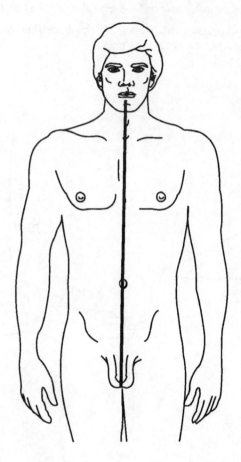

1CV: *Entry point*
Located on the floor of the pelvis, between the anus and the genitalia.

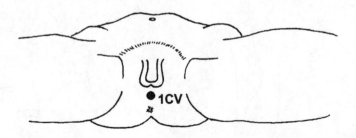

2CV: Located above the pubis. Effective in treating gynaecological disorders.

3CV: *Mo point of the Bladder*
Located on the median line running across the lower abdomen, 1 finger-breadth above the pubis.
Cystitis (-).
Incontinence (+).

4CV: *Mo point of the Small intestine*
Located 1 thumb's breadth above point 3CV.
Colitis (-).
Defective assimilation (+).

5CV: *Mo point of the Lower Triple Heater*
Located 1 thumb's breadth above point 4CV.
Sexual stimulant (+).

6CV: *Master point governing Energy*
Located 2 fingerbreadths below the navel.

8CV: Located in the navel
Snoring (+, or even better, applying heat to the point).

9CV: Located 1 fingerbreadth above the navel.
Distributes water around the body.

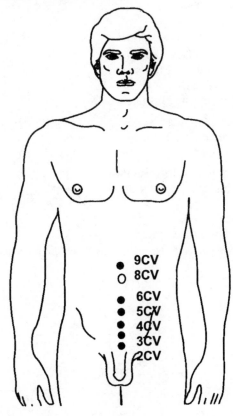

12CV: *Mo point of the Medium Triple Heater and the Stomach*
Located halfway between the navel and the xiphisternum. Central point facilitating digestion and balance. Strengthens the body. Helps energy recovery after exertion or during convalescence.
Sluggish digestion (+).
Weariness (+).
Stomach cramps and heartburn (-).

14CV: *Mo point for the Heart*
Located 6 fingerbreadths above the navel and 1 fingerbreadth below the sternum.
Anxiety (+).
Tachycardia (-).

15CV: *Solar plexus point*
Located below the tip of the sternum.
Spasms of the solar plexus (-).

17CV: *Mo point of the Upper Triple Heater*
Located on the sternum between the breasts.
Regulates respiration.
Introversion (-).
Wind (-).

22CV: Located in the hollow above the fork in the sternum. Effective in treating the thyroid.
To get rid of coughing fits (-).

23CV: Located above the Adam's apple.
Abundant salivation (-).
Sore throat (-).

24CV: Located in a hollow between the tip of the chin and the lower lip.
Torticollis (-).
Dental neuralgia (-).
Excessive thirst in diabetics (-).

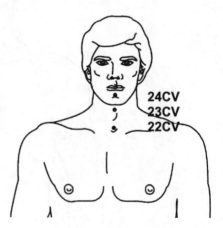

Governing EV

Polarity:	Yang.
Description:	This vessel represents the sea of yang PMs.
	Just like the Conception Vessel, as well as being an Extraordinary Vessel with a key opening point, the Governing Vessel disposes of its own points. It is median and therefore unilateral.
Symptoms:	Pain along the course of the Governing EV (along the spine and the median line over the skull and the forehead).
	Backache.
	Torticollis.
	Cervical arthrosis.
	General exhaustion.
	Instability.
	Nervous tension.
Treatment:	Disperse points 3SI, 62B, 1GV and 26GV.
Key point:	3SI
Partner point:	62B
Entry point:	1GV
Exit point:	26GV

Position of points

3SI: Located on the inner side of the hand, in a small hollow touching the bony protuberance of the metacarpal/phalanx joint, ie, at the end of the crease formed when the hand is closed.

62B: Located below the lateral malleolus.

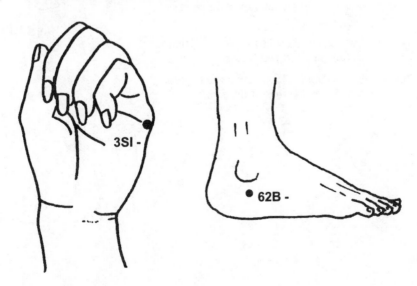

1GV: Located on the tip of the coccyx.

26GV: Located in the hollow just below the nose.

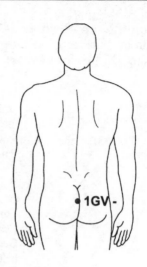

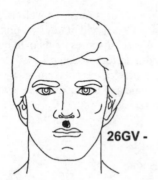

Disorders connected with the Governing EV

Pain along the spine

Begin by stimulating the Governing EV, including points 4GV, 9GV, 14GV and 20GV. In addition, stimulate points:

3SI-, 62B-, 1GV-, 4GV+, 9GV-, 14GV-, 20GV- and 26GV-, then disperse any painful points that remain.

4GV: Located in the hollow of the back, level with the kidneys, between the second and third lumbar vertebrae.

9GV: Located between the seventh and eighth dorsal vertebrae, almost in the centre of the back.

14GV: Located between the first dorsal vertebra and the last cervical vertebra.

20GV: Located on the top of the head, on a line connecting the tops of the ears.

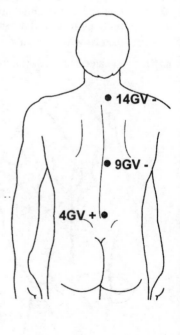

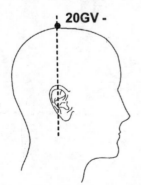

Pain on the top of the head

Begin by stimulating the Governing EV, including point 20GV and ending with point 1K, in other words:

3SI-, 62B-, 1GV-, 20GV-, 26GV- and 1K+.

20GV: Located on the top of the head, on a line connecting the tops of the ears.

1K: Located on the sole of the foot, between the two muscle masses.

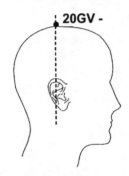

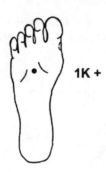

Cervical arthrosis

After stimulating the points along the Governing EV, ie, points 3SI-, 62B-, 1GV- and 26GV-, add the following points, if necessary:

54B-, 67B+, 10B-, 44GB+, 20GB-, 14GV- and 20GV-.

54B: Located right in the centre of the back of the knee.

67B: Located at the outer corner of the small toenail.

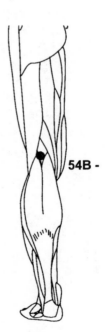

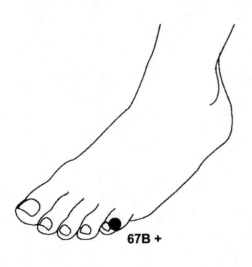

10B: Located at the back of the neck below the occipital protuberances.

44GB: Located at the outer corner of the fourth toenail.

20GB: Located at the back of the neck, below the occipital protuberances.

14GV: Located between the first dorsal vertebra and the last cervical vertebra.

20GV: Located on the top of the head, on a line connecting the tops of the ears.

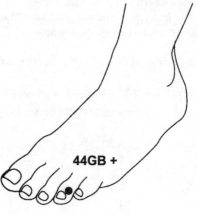

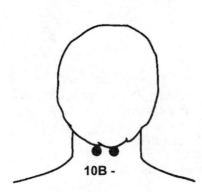

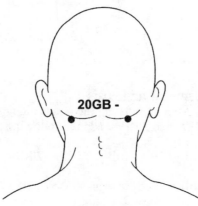

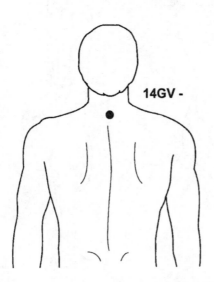

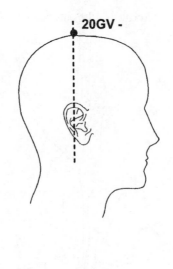

Torticollis

After stimulating the points along the Governing EV, ie, points 3SI-, 62B-, 1GV- and 26GV-, add the following points, if necessary:

5Sp+, 60B-, 54B-, 10B-, 34GB-, 1TH+, 4TH- and 10TH-.

5Sp: Located in front of the medial malleolus, on the front of the foot, inside the peroneous longus tendon, in the hollow formed when the foot is turned inwards.

60B: Located behind the lateral malleolus.

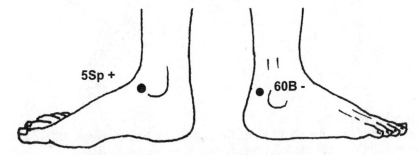

54B: Located right in the centre of the back of the knee.

10B: Located at the back of the neck, below the occipital protuberances.

34GB: Located below the outer side of the knee, below the top of the fibula, the small bony bump you can feel just below the knee, slightly to the rear.

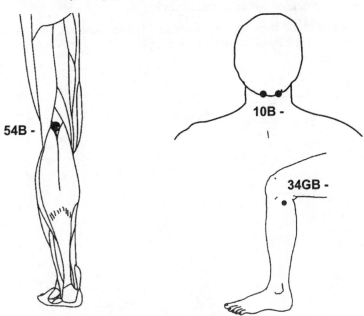

1TH: Located on the outer side of the fourth fingernail.

4TH: Located in the crease on the back of the wrist.

10TH: Located above the tip of the olecranon, ie, behind the elbow.

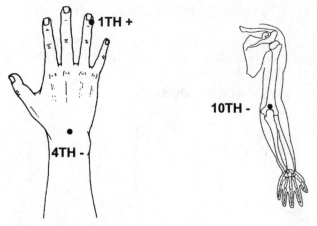

General weariness

After stimulating the points along the Governing EV, ie, points 3SI-, 62B-, 1GV- and 26GV-, add the following points, if necessary:

36S+, 4LI+, 9L+, 12CV+, 7K+, 23B+, 4GV+, 8Lv+ and 4LI+, all to be boosted, preferably in the morning.

36S: Located 4 fingerbreadths below the knee, between the peroneous longus and the extensor digitorum communis longus.

4LI: Located in the angle formed by the first two metacarpals, in front of and touching the base of the second metacarpal.

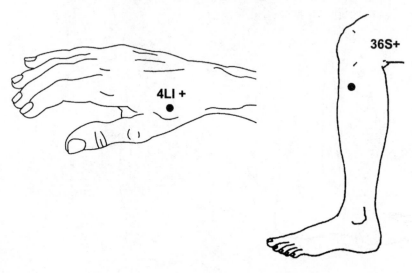

9L: Located in the radial groove, on the wrist crease, ie, before the radial styloid.

12CV: Located halfway between the navel and the xiphisternum.

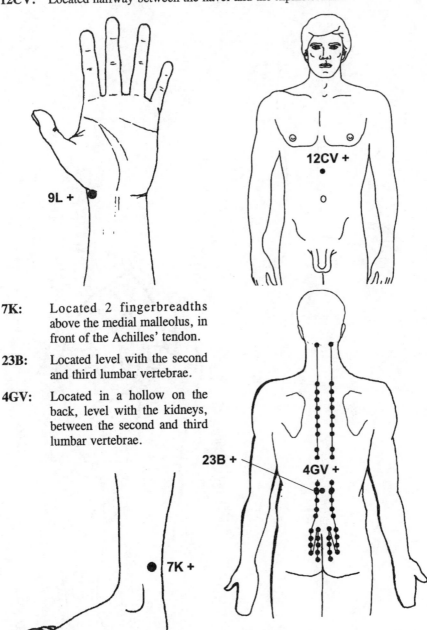

7K: Located 2 fingerbreadths above the medial malleolus, in front of the Achilles' tendon.

23B: Located level with the second and third lumbar vertebrae.

4GV: Located in a hollow on the back, level with the kidneys, between the second and third lumbar vertebrae.

8Lv: Located on the inside of the knee crease, touching the joint.

4LI: Located on the outer edge of the hand, in a small hollow just before the wrist bones.

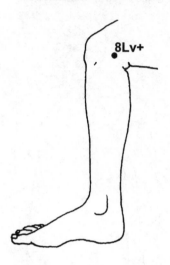

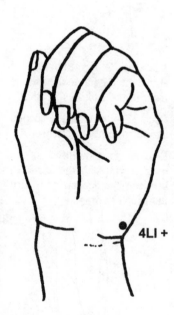

Governing Vessel

Polarity: Yang.
Course: The Governing Vessel begins at the tip of the coccyx, runs all the way up the spine and over the top of the head to end below the nose.

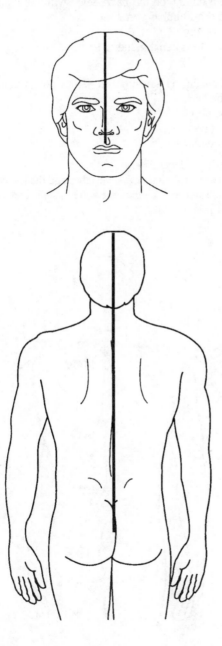

1GV: *Entry point*
Located on the tip of the coccyx.
Haemorrhoids (-).
Pain along the spine (+).

4GV: *Menn Ming point or the Gateway to Life*
Located in a hollow on the back, level with the kidneys and between the second and third lumbar vertebrae.
Weakened virility (+).
To stimulate the adrenal glands (+).
To invigorate (+).

9GV: Located between the seventh and eighth dorsal vertebrae, almost in the centre of the back.
Listlessness (+).
Rheumatism (+).
Lack of strength (+).

14GV: *Junction point of Yang Energy*
Located between the first dorsal vertebra and the last cervical vertebra. This point can be 'saturated' by the time you reach the end of a hard day. Disperse this point if it is painful.
Torticollis (-).
Chills (+).

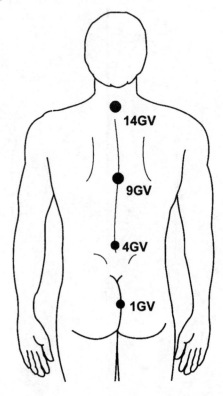

Points 19GV and 20GV are connected with cosmic waves and encourage concentration and sleep.

19GV: Located on the top of the head, level with the join between the parietal and occipital bones.

20GV: Located on the top of the head, on a line joining the tops of the ears.
To soothe tension (-).
To encourage concentration (+).

24GV: Located on the hairline.
Sinusitis (-).

25GV: Located on the tip of the nose.
Intoxication point (-).

26GV: *Life and Death point*
Exit point
Located in the hollow just below the nose. A heavy blow administered to this point can cause death whereas when it is boosted, it can revive an unconscious person.

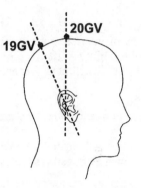

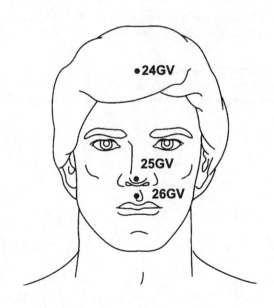

CHAPTER 5

Ailments and their treatments

Anxiety

Anxiety is often the result of an energy imbalance brought on by stress and by a lack of internal energy stability. The cure consists of raising the threshold of invulnerability in the face of stress and increasing self-confidence. Here are the points that will help you achieve this:

Boost point: 6CV;
Disperse points: 3H, 3Lv and 4LI.

6CV: Located on the median line of the abdomen, 3 fingerbreadths below the navel.

3H: Located on the crease formed when the elbow is bent, level with the joint.

3Lv: Located at the tip of the angle formed by the first two metatarsals when the toes are spread.

4LI: Located in the angle formed by the first two metacarpals, touching the base of the second metacarpal.

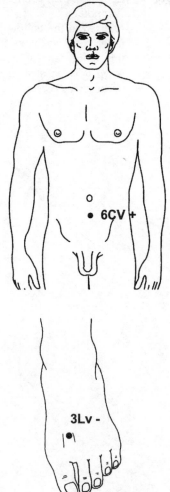

6CV +

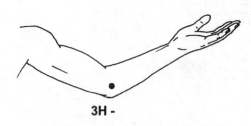

3H -

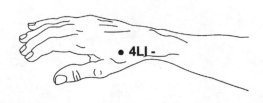

4LI -

3Lv -

Appetite (Excessive)

There can be several reasons for excessive appetite. It could be due to a lack of affection, but is more often caused by a need for vitamins and trace elements that our overrefined diet does not provide in sufficient quantity for our body's needs.

A good way of avoiding this condition is to take 3 Brewers' yeast tablets 15 minutes before each meal. This type of yeast is particularly rich in B-group vitamins and can therefore satisfy the body's needs, thus encouraging the subject to eat less.

Disperse point: 45S, 36S and 12CV.

45S: Located at the outer corner of the second toenail, alongside the third toe.

36S: Located 4 fingerbreadths below the knee, close to the tibia.

12CV: Located halfway between the navel and the tip of the sternum.

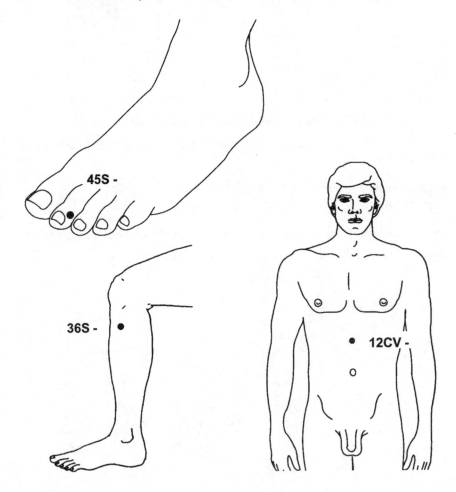

Appetite (Insufficient)

Boost points: 41S and 12CV.

41S: Located in a hollow in the middle of the front of the ankle, between the two tendons.

12CV: Located halfway between the navel and the tip of the sternum.

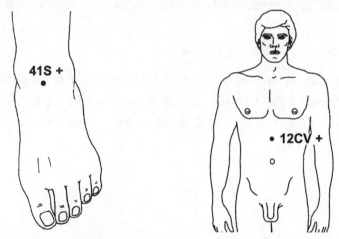

Arteritis (Inflammation of an artery)

This treatment does not claim to cure arteritis, but it can definitely help soothe the condition.

Disperse points: 6MH, 32S, 3Lv and 9L.
Boost points: 39GB and 4H.

6MH: Located 3 fingerbreadths above the wrist crease, between the two tendons.

32S: Located right in the centre of the front of the thigh.

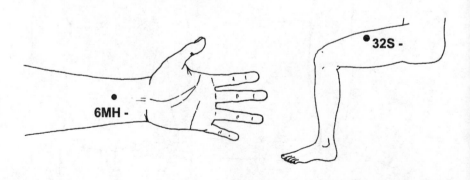

3Lv: Located at the tip of the angle formed by the first two metatarsals when the toes are spread.

9L: Located in the radial groove, on the wrist crease, in other words in front of the radial styloid.

39GB: Located 2 fingerbreadths above the lateral malleolus, on the fibula.

4H: Located on the outer edge of the inside of the wrist, in the groove just before the styloid (small pointed bone).

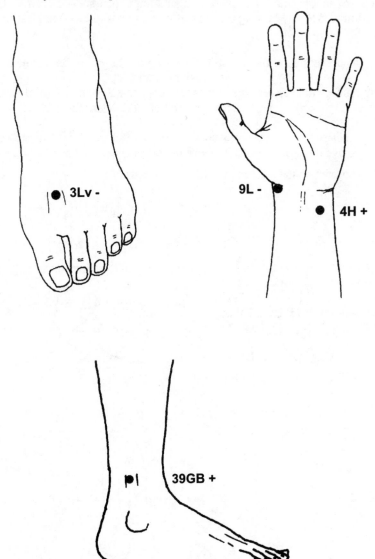

Asthma

These few points can abort an asthma attack.

Disperse point: 7L;
Boost point: 17CV (unless the subject is too nervous).

Here is a formula you can use and which sometimes gives good results. Drop 15 drops of macerated garlic onto a sugar lump, then suck it slowly. Garlic maceration is made by leaving 6 cloves of garlic to soak in a large glass of 90% alcohol for a fortnight.

Recommended essential oil: Mint (one drop on the tip of the tongue as soon as coughing begins).
Recommended trace elements: Manganese-copper-magnesium-lithium and manganese-cobalt, alternately.

7L: Located in the radial groove where you can feel the pulse, 3 fingerbreadths above the wrist crease, ie, above the radial styloid (a bone in the wrist).

17CV: Located on the sternum, between the breasts.

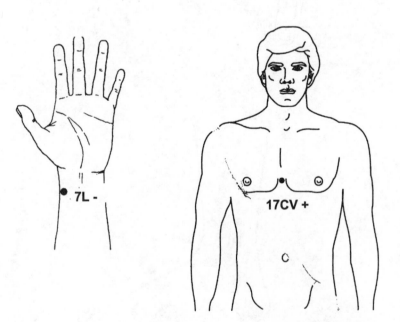

Arteriosclerosis (Hardening of the arteries)

Disperse points: 6Sp, 3Lv, 14Lv, 39GB, 62B, 8MH and 36S.

An accumulation of fatty plaques in the arteries reduces their elasticity and leads to hardening of the arteries, the major cause of death in the Western World.

Eliminate: Tobacco, alcohol, animal fats, sugar, pork preparations.
Consume: Vegetables, salads, fruit, garlic, onions. Lemons. Grapefruit. Cold-pressed virgin vegetable oils, preferably sunflower or olive oils.
Recommended: Infusions of dandelion roots. Horseradish juice. Grapefruit juice.
Keep an eye on: Cholesterol and fat levels in the blood.
Recommended trace elements: Selenium, chromium.

6Sp: Located on the inside of the leg, 4 fingerbreadths above the medial malleolus, in a hollow behind the tibia.

3Lv: Located on the upper side of the foot, at the tip of the angle formed by the first two metatarsals when the toes are spread, touching the bone of the big toe.

14Lv: Located between the sixth and seventh ribs, directly below the nipple.

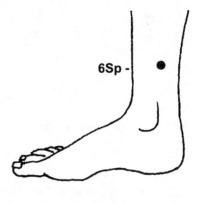

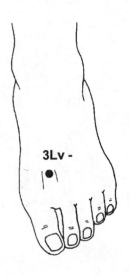

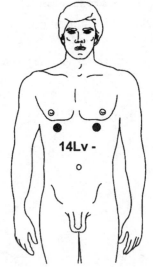

39GB: Located 2 fingerbreadths above the lateral malleolus, on the fibula.

62B: Located below the lateral malleolus.

8MH: Located right in the centre of the palm of the hand, on the transversal crease.

36S: Located 4 fingerbreadths below the knee, close to the tibia.

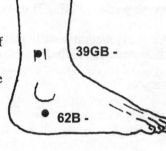

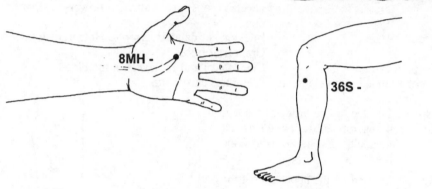

Bravery

To lend courage stimulate the following points:

Boost points: 1K, 7K and 23B.

1K: Located on the sole of the foot, between the two muscle masses.

7K: Located 2 fingerbreadths above the medial malleolus, in front of the Achilles' tendon.

23B: Located level with the second and third lumbar vertebrae.

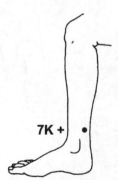

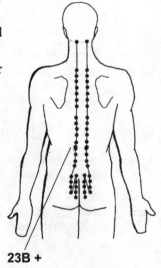

Burns

Disperse point: 7L and the area around the burn.

Point 7L is capable of rapidly soothing minor burns. I also recommend you place the burned area in a basin of cold water with a small amount of kaolin. In the case of severe burns, consult a doctor.

7L: Located in the radial groove where you can feel the pulse, 3 fingerbreadths above the wrist crease, ie, above the radial styloid.

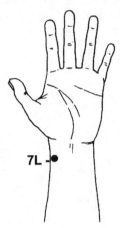

Chilblains

Avoid heating up cold extremities using a source of intense heat or hot water-bottles. Take brewer's yeast, wheat germ and wheat germ oil. Make up a poultice at night using wheat germ oil.

Recommended trace elements: Chromium,
                                 manganese-copper-magnesium-lithium,
                                 sulphur.

The following points should be dispersed on the affected side and boosted on the opposite side, *when only one side is affected*.

Chilblains on the fingers

Disperse points: 2TH and Tchang Tou.

2TH: Located between the fourth and little fingers, just below the joint.

Tchang
Tou: Located between the middle and the index fingers, just before the joint, slightly to the index finger side.

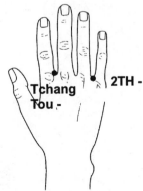

Chilblains on the toes

Disperse point: 39S once a day for a week, then once or twice a week for three weeks.

39S: Located on the outer side of the leg, 4 fingerbreadths above the lateral malleolus.

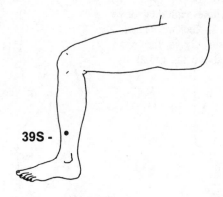

Chills

Boost points: 1LI, 4LI, 11L, 7K, 12CV and 1L.

1LI: Located at the corner of the index fingernail, alongside the thumb.

4LI: Located in the angle formed by the first two metacarpals, touching the base of the second metacarpal.

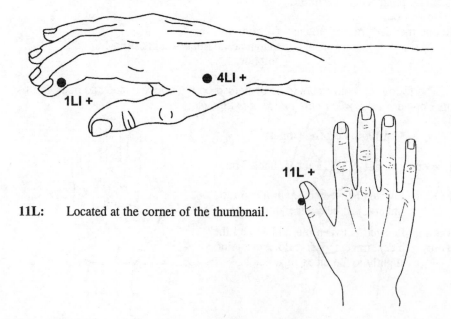

11L: Located at the corner of the thumbnail.

7K: Located 2 fingerbreadths above the medial malleolus, in front of the Achilles' tendon.

12CV: Located halfway between the navel and the xiphisternum.

1L: Located on the upper side of the second rib, below point 2L, from which it is separated by the first rib.

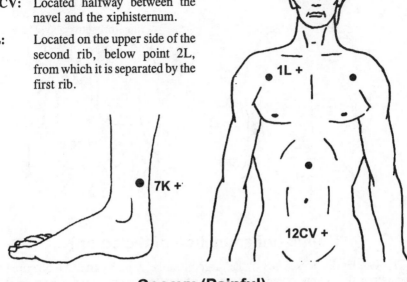

Coccyx (Painful)

If the coccyx is displaced due to a fall, it can remain painful until it is repositioned by a specialist in manipulating bones (osteopath, chiropractor).

The following points can help relieve a painful coccyx:

Disperse points: 3SI and 62B;
Boost points: 1GV and 26GV.

3SI: Located just below the metacarpal/phalanx joint.

62B: Located below the lateral malleolus.

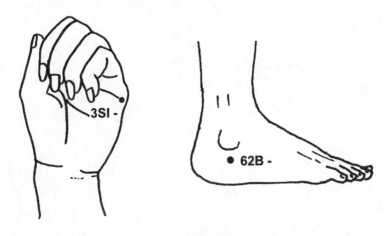

1GV: Located at the tip of the coccyx.

26GV: Located in the hollow just below the nose.

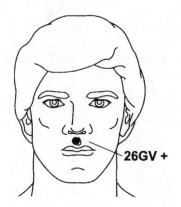

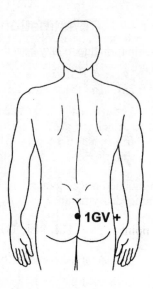

26GV +

1GV +

Colitis (Inflammation of the colon)

This can be due to spasms in the large intestine, which can often be cured by stimulating the points given. But we must not forget that severe pain may be caused by appendicitis which can require urgent surgery. When in doubt, a quick visit to the doctor is necessary. But if the pain turns out to be a false alarm, the stimulation of the following points can often be surprisingly effective:

Disperse points: 6MH, 9Sp and 9LI.

6MH: Located 2 fingerbreadths above the inner wrist crease.

9Sp: Located below the inside of the knee, touching the bony tibia/knee angle.

9LI: Located on the outside of the forearm, 4 fingerbreadths below the elbow crease.

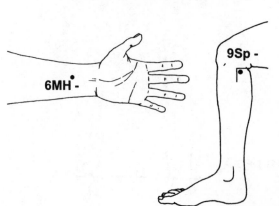

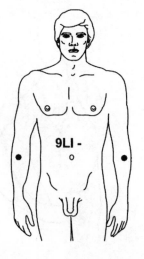

6MH -

9Sp -

9LI -

Constipation (Due to lazy bowels)

Constipation due to lazy bowels is in fact a functional deficiency of the colon. Stools are few and far between, normal or larger in size. The abdominal muscles can also lack vigour.

Avoid:	Chocolate, sugar, meat, sausages and patés.
Eat:	Vegetables, salads dressed with cold-pressed virgin vegetable oil, wholegrain cereals (rice, millet, barley), wholemeal pasta, fruit (except quince).
Recommended trace element:	Magnesium.
Recommended vitamin:	B5 (pantothenic acid).

Boost points: 1LI, 4LI, 11LI and 25S.

1LI: Located at the corner of the index fingernail, alongside the thumb.

4LI: Located at the tip of the angle formed by the first two metacarpals (thumb and index finger bones), when the fingers are spread.

11LI: Located at the outermost point of the crease formed when the elbow is bent.

25S: Located 3 fingerbreadths outside the navel.

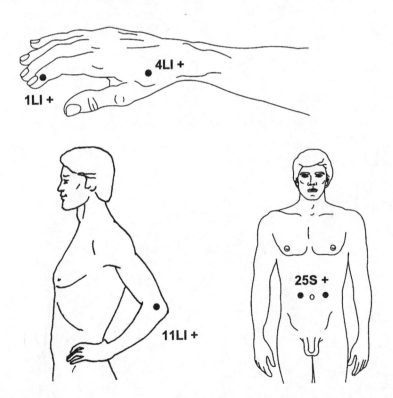

Constipation (Due to spasms)

Constipation due to spasms – exactly the opposite problem to constipation due to lazy bowels – is the result of exaggerated contraction of the colon. Stools are small, as if strangled.

Disperse points: 6MH, 9Sp, 2LI and 4LI.

Recommended trace elements: Cobalt, magnesium, manganese-cobalt.
Recommended vitamin: B5 (pantothenic acid).

6MH: Located 3 fingerbreadths above the wrist crease, between the two tendons.

9Sp: Located below the inside of the knee, touching the tibia/knee bony joint.

2LI: Located just below the metacarpal/phalanx joint, on the inside of the index finger.

4LI: Located at the tip of the angle formed by the first two metacarpals (thumb and index finger bones), when the fingers are spread.

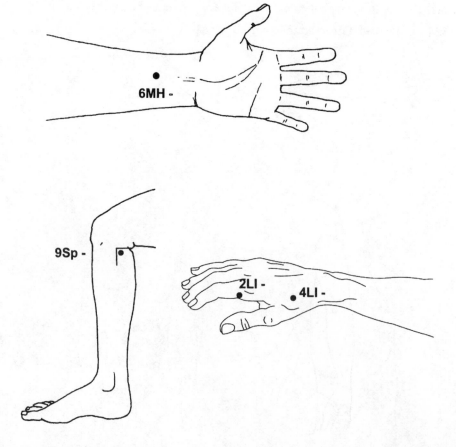

Convalescence

The following points will assist the rapid recovery of your strength after an illness, an operation or an accident.

Boost points: 12CV, 6Sp and 39GB.

12CV: Located in the centre of the abdomen, halfway between the navel and the xiphisternum.

6Sp: Located on the inside of the leg, 4 fingerbreadths above the medial malleolus, in a hollow behind the tibia.

39GB: Located 2 fingerbreadths above the lateral malleolus, on the fibula.

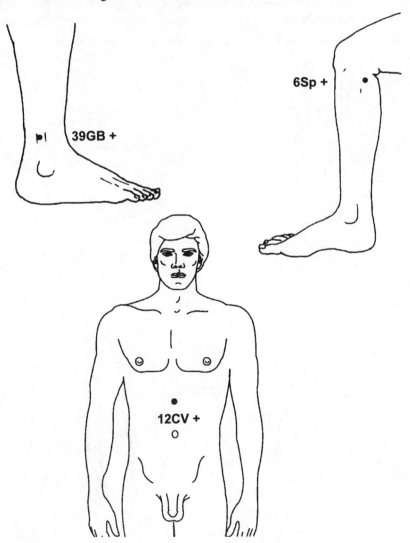

Coughs

Disperse points: 7L and 22CV;
Boost points: 7K and 23B.

Recommended essential oil: Mint (as an inhalation).
Recommended trace element: Manganese-cobalt.
Recommended vitamin: C.

7L: Located in the radial groove where you can feel the pulse, 3 fingerbreadths above the wrist crease.

22CV: Located in the hollow just above where the sternum forks.

7K: Located 2 fingerbreadths above the medial malleolus, in front of the Achilles' tendon.

23B: Located level with the second and third lumbar vertebrae.

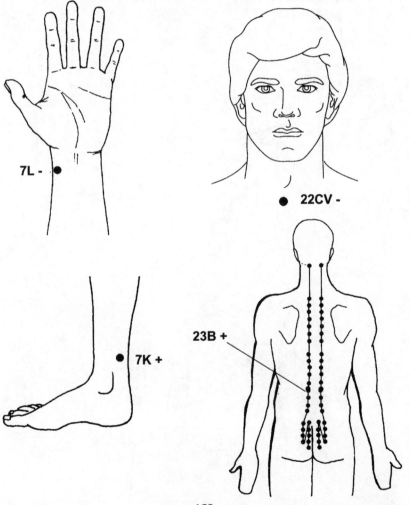

Cramp (In the calf muscle)

Cramp can be caused by a number of different factors. It could be due to calcium and potassium metabolic disorders, or to circulation problems; but the main cause is muscular fatigue. The following points will help you get rid of cramp rapidly.

Disperse points: 34GB, 57B and 3Lv.

Recommended trace elements: Calcium, magnesium, manganese-cobalt.
Recommended vitamin: B2.

34GB: Located below the outer knee, below the head of the fibula, the small bony bump one can feel just below the knee, slightly to the rear.

57B: Located at the back of the leg, just below the calf muscles.

3Lv: Located on the upper side of the foot, at the tip of the angle formed by the first two metatarsals when the toes are spread, touching the big toe bone.

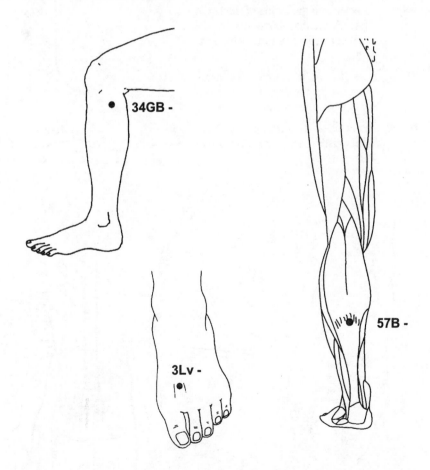

Diabetes

Diabetes is a serious disorder which must be closely supervised by a doctor. Diabetics must follow a sugar-free diet and they are advised to eat vegetables, salads, wholemeal cereals, lentils, mushrooms, pumpkin, yoghurt, cheese, walnuts, almonds, fruit (particularly acid fruits such as berries, cherries, acid apples, myrtles, raspberries, strawberries, avoiding fruit that is very sweet, such as dates).

Here are the points that can help treat diabetes:

Disperse points: 4Sp, 6Sp, 3Lv and 6MH;
Boost points: 7K and 23B.

Recommended trace elements: Chromium, cobalt, zinc-nickel-cobalt.

4Sp: Located in the centre of the inside of the foot, on the line between the sole of the foot and the dorsal skin.

6Sp: Located on the inside of the leg, 4 fingerbreadths above the medial malleolus, in a hollow behind the tibia.

3Lv: Located at the tip of the angle formed by the first two metatarsals when the toes are spread.

6MH: Located 3 fingerbreadths above the wrist crease, between the two tendons.

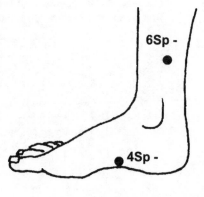

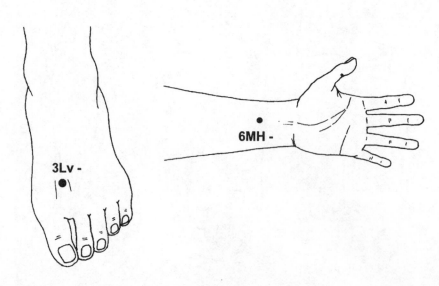

7K: Located 2 fingerbreadths above the inner ankle bone, in front of the Achilles' tendon.

23B: Located level with the second and third lumbar vertebrae.

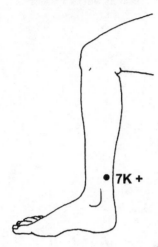

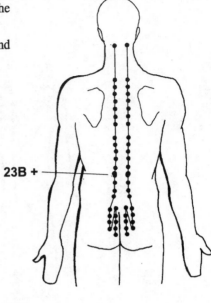

Diarrhoea

If you are suffering from yin diarrhoea due to a chill or to a lack of general vigour, stimulate the following points:

Boost points: 37S, 7K and 23B.

Recommended essential oil: Savory.

37S: Located in the middle of the front of the lower leg, behind the tibia, 8 fingerbreadths below the knee or 8 fingerbreadths above the lateral malleolus.

7K: Located 2 fingerbreadths above the medial malleolus, in front of the Achilles' tendon.

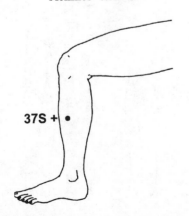

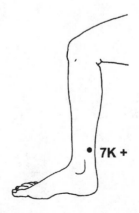

23B: Located level with the second and third lumbar vertebrae.

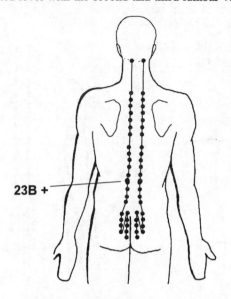

23B +

Digestion (Slow and heavy)

Boost points: 36S, 41S and 12CV.

Recommended essential oil: Mint.
Recommended plants: Tarragon, basil, rosemary.

36S: Located 4 fingerbreadths below the knee, close to the tibia.

41S: Located right in the centre of the instep, in the hollow between the tendons.

12CV: Located in the middle of the abdomen, halfway between the navel and the xiphisternum.

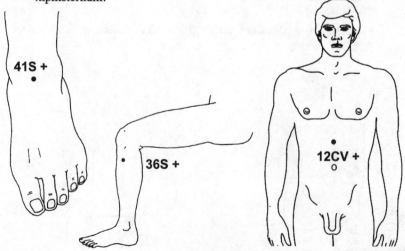

41S +

36S +

12CV +

Dissatisfaction (General)

Boost points: 9L, 4LI and 7K;
Disperse point: 40GB.

9L: Located in the radial groove, on the wrist crease, ie, before the radial styloid.

4LI: Located in the angle formed by the first two metacarpals, touching the front of the second metacarpal.

7K: Located 2 fingerbreadths above the medial malleolus, in front of the Achilles' tendon.

40GB: Located at the instep, in a hollow just in front of the lateral malleolus.

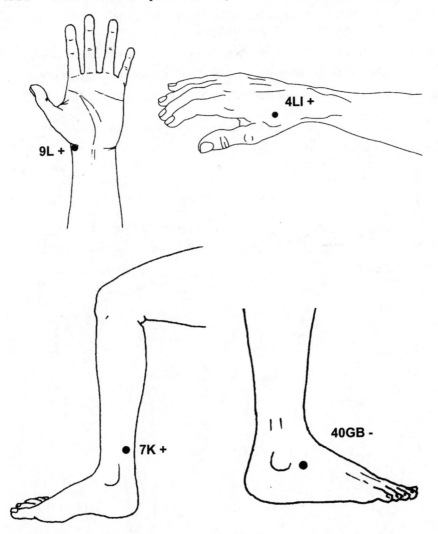

Dizziness

A medical examination should always be carried out to determine the cause of such an energy imbalance. However, the stimulation of the following points can be very effective in certain cases:

Disperse points: 62B and 3SI;
Boost point: 4LI;
Disperse point: 20GB;
Boost points: 19GV and 20GV.

62B: Located below the lateral malleolus.

3SI: Located just after the metacarpal/phalanx joint.

4LI: Located in the angle formed by the first two metacarpals, touching the front of the base of the second metacarpal.

20GB: Located at the back of the neck, below the occipital protuberances.

19GV: Located on the top of the head, level with the parietal/occipital join.

20GV: Located on the top of the head, on a line joining the tops of the ears.

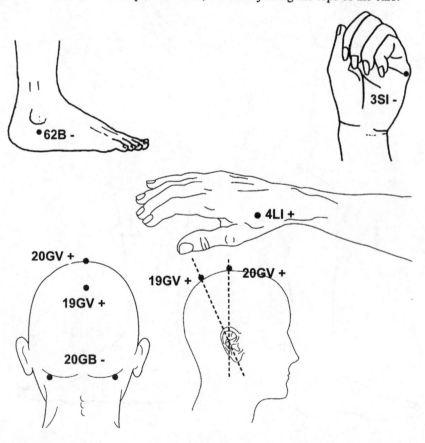

Eczema

Eczema is often an allergic reaction to a substance or a foreign body that the body is striving to reject. There are a host of causes. Certain individuals have a predisposition to eczema but, in any event, it is important to eliminate the source of the allergy and particularly to avoid eating sugar, pork and animal fats, among other things.

Recommended infusion: Wild pansy (2 infusions per day, using 20 g of fresh flowers and leaves per litre of water).
Recommended trace elements: Magnesium, sulphur.
Recommended vitamins: A, E, F (cold-pressed virgin vegetable oil).

Boost points: 54B, 8Lv and 11LI.
Disperse point: 13B.

54B: Located right in the middle of the back of the knee.

8Lv: Located on the inside crease behind the knee, touching the joint.

11LI: Located at the outermost point of the crease, formed when the elbow is bent.

13B: Located level with the third and fourth dorsal vertebrae.

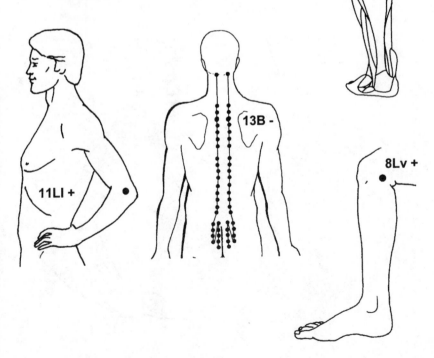

165

Elbow (Painful)

If the pain is on the same side as the thumb, the problem is 'tennis elbow'.

Boost point: 1LI;
Disperse point: 11LI and the painful points;
Boost point: 13GB.

1LI: Located at the corner of the index fingernail, alongside the thumb.

11LI: Located on the outside of the elbow crease.

13GB: Located just on the hairline, directly above the outer corner of the eye.

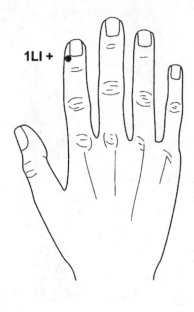

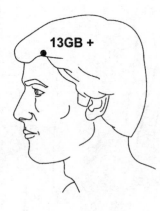

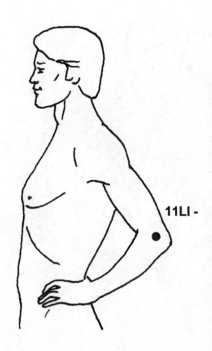

Elbow (Painful)

If the pain is on the same side as little finger, the problem is 'golf elbow'.

Boost points: 1SI and 3SI;
Disperse point: 8LI and the painful points;
Boost point: 13GB.

1SI: Located at the outer corner of the little fingernail.

3SI: Located just after the metacarpal/phalanx joint.

8LI: Located just behind the elbow, on the inside, in a small groove.

13GB: Located just on the hairline, directly above the outer corner of the eye.

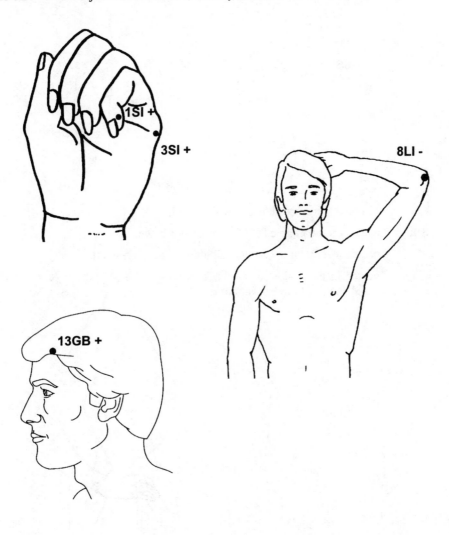

Energy (Lack of)

Boost points: 36S, 6Sp and 6CV;
Disperse point: 38B;
Boost points: 23B and 4GV.

Recommended plants: Ginseng, savory, rosemary.

36S: Located 4 fingerbreadths below the knee, between the peroneous longus and the extensor digitorum communis longus.

6Sp: Located on the inside of the leg, 4 fingerbreadths above the medial malleolus, in a hollow behind the tibia.

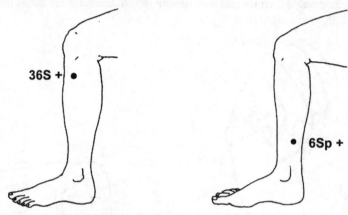

6CV: Located 2 fingerbreadths below the navel.

38B: Located on the inner edge of the shoulder-blade.

23B: Located level with the second and third lumbar vertebrae.

4GV: Located in the hollow of the back, level with the kidneys, between the second and third lumbar vertebrae.

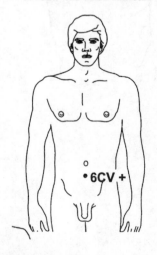
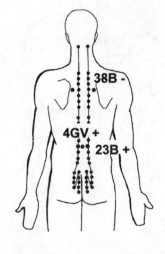

168

Eyes (Sore)

If your eyes are red due to tiredness or an allergy, stimulating the following points may help:

Disperse points: 6MH, 1S, 1GB, 38GB, 10GB and 3SI.
Boost points: 3Lv, 4LI and 23GV.

6MH: Located 3 fingerbreadths above the wrist crease, between the two tendons.

1S: Located right in the centre of the hollow below the eye.

1GB: Located at the outer corner of the eye.

38GB: Located 4 fingerbreadths above the lateral malleolus, in a small hollow on the front edge of the fibula.

10GB: Located above and behind the pinna.

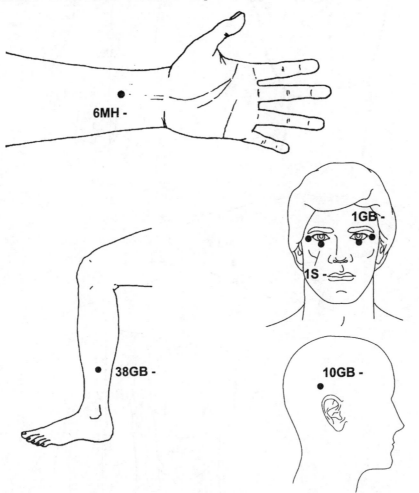

3SI: Located just below the metacarpal/phalanx joint.

3Lv: Located on the foot, at the tip of the angle formed by the first two metatarsals when the toes are spread, touching the big toe bone.

4LI: Located at the tip of the angle formed by the first two metacarpals (thumb and index finger bones) when the fingers are spread.

23GV: Located on the median line of the forehead, on the hairline.

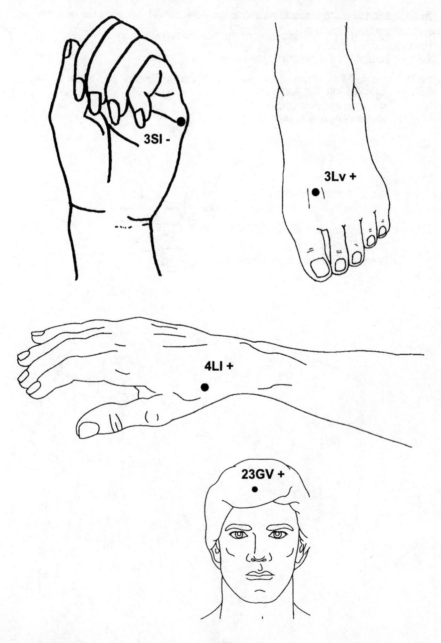

Eyesight (To ímprove)

You should, of course, consult an optician with regard to eyesight problems. However, the stimulation of these points can improve vision in general.

Boost points: 6SI, 3Lv, 18B, 23B, 20GB, 19GV, 20GV, 10GB, 11GB and 12GB.

Recommended trace element: Selenium.
Recommended vitamins: A, B2, C.
Recommended food: Carrot juice.
                           Myrtles.

6SI: Located on the inner side of the wrist, in a hollow one fingerbreadth above the wrist bone.

3Lv: Located just after the metacarpal/phalanx joint.

18B: Located level with the ninth and tenth dorsal vertebrae, 2 fingerbreadths outside the median line.

23B: Located level with the second and third lumbar vertebrae, 2 fingerbreadths from the median line.

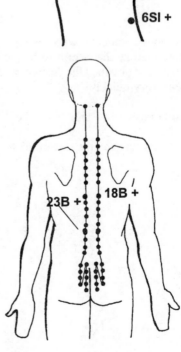

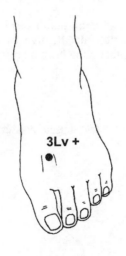

171

20GB: Located at the back of the neck, below the occipital protuberances.

19GV: Located on the top of the head, level with the join between the parietal and occipital bones.

20GV: Located on the top of the head, on a line joining the tops of the ears.

10 GB: Located above and behind the ear.

11GB: Located behind the ear, directly below point 10GB.

12GB: Located half a thumb's breadth behind the ear, on the lower edge of the occipital bone, behind the jawbone.

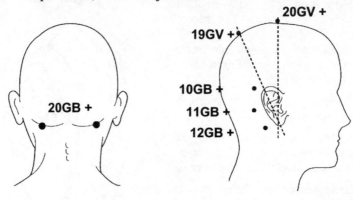

Fainting

To revive someone who has fainted, just one of these points can be enough. Choose the one that seems to be the easiest to stimulate. If, after two minutes, you have not obtained the desired results, try another point because results should be seen very quickly.

Boost points: 1K, 4LI or 26GV.

1K: Located on the sole of the foot, between the two muscle masses.

4LI: Located at the tip of the angle formed by the first two metacarpals (the thumb and index finger bones) when the fingers are spread.

26GV: Located in the hollow just below the nose.

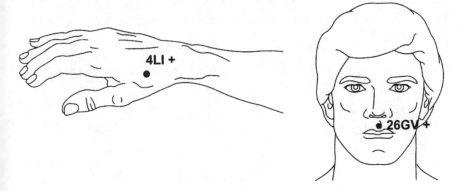

Fatigue

Boost points: 12CV, 6CV, 36S, 6Sp and 9L.

Recommended essential oil: Savory (rubbed into the lumbar region of the back, after showering in the morning).

Recommended trace elements:
  Evening weariness: Manganese-copper-magnesium-lithium.
  Morning tiredness: Copper-gold-silver.

12CV: Located halfway between the navel and the tip of the sternum.

6CV: Located 2 fingerbreadths below the navel.

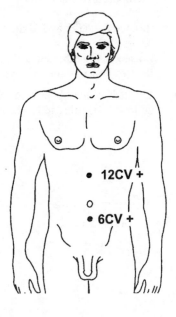

173

36S: Located 4 fingerbreadths below the knee, between the peroneous longus and the extensor digitorum communis longus.

6Sp: Located on the inside of the leg, 4 fingerbreadths above the medial malleolus, in a hollow behind the tibia.

9L: Located in the radial groove, on the wrist crease, ie, before the radial styloid.

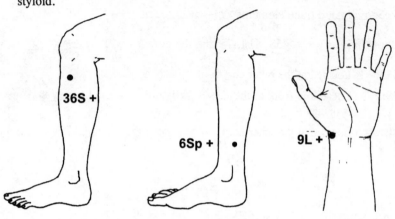

Fever

Fever is the result of the body's fight against germs and viruses. It is therefore a necessary process. But it can sometimes go on for too long or can be too intense, in which case you should stimulate the following two points, which can help to lower the temperature rapidly:

Disperse points: 5TH and 10Sp.

5TH: Located 2 fingerbreadths above the crease on the back of the wrist, between the two bones of the forearm.

10Sp: Located on the upper side of the thigh; slightly towards the inside, in a hollow 4 fingerbreadths above the knee.

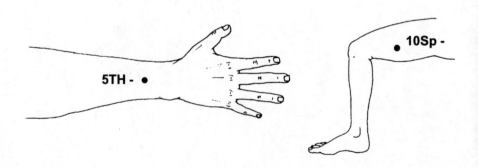

Gums (To strengthen)

If we want to keep our teeth healthy, it is very important to take good care of our gums, ensuring that tartar does not take hold. A piece of advice: always rinse your mouth with salty water after each meal and make sure you don't forget to rinse again before going to bed.

Recommended trace elements: Magnesium, silica.

Boost points: 45S, 1LI, 7S and the gums.

45S: Located at the outer corner of the second toenail.

7S: Located in front of the ear, in the hollow that can be seen when the mouth is opened.

1LI: Located at the inner corner of the index fingernail, alongside the thumb.

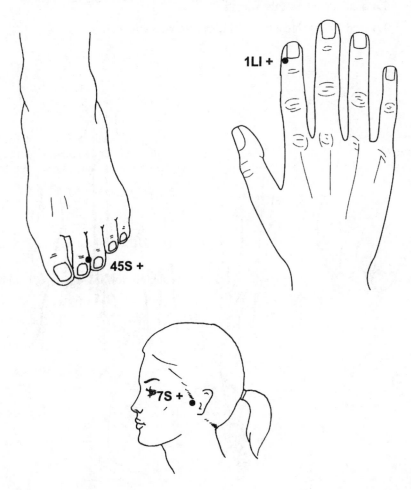

Haemorrhoids

If you suffer this painful condition, bowel movements should be made easier by eating sufficient vegetables, fruit, salads, wholegrain cereals and cold-pressed virgin vegetable oil. Here are the points that, when stimulated, will relieve you immediately, and which may help avoid surgery in particularly bad cases.

Boost point: 1Sp.
Disperse points: 57B, 1GV and 28B.

Recommended essential oil: Cypress (applied directly to the haemorrhoids).
Recommended vitamins: A, E.

1Sp: Located at the inner corner of the big toenail.

57B: Located on the back of the leg, just below the calf muscle.

1GV: Located at the tip of the coccyx.

28B: Located 2 fingerbreadths outside the second sacral hollow.

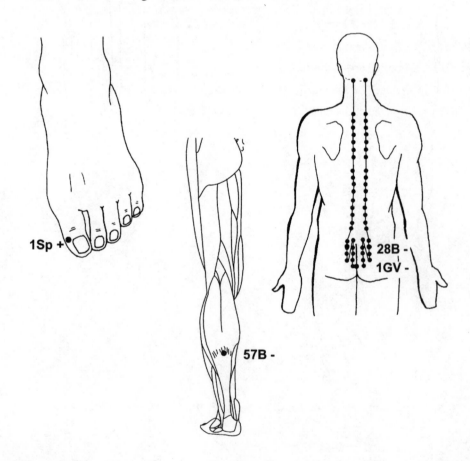

Head cold

The common cold, with inflammation of the nose and throat, can be due to any one of more than 200 viruses. People are far more likely to catch colds when they are tired or poisoned by a diet rich in toxins and poor in vitamins and trace elements. A runny nose can also be caused by allergies. Whatever the cause, the same points should be stimulated:

Disperse point: 7L;
Boost points: 4LI, 20LI, 23CV, 8Lv and 67B.

Recommended essential oils: Marjoram, mint.
Recommended trace elements: Iodine, manganese-copper-magnesium-lithium, sulphur.
Recommended vitamin: C.

7L: Located in the radial groove where you can feel the pulse, 3 fingerbreadths above the wrist crease, ie, above the radial styloid bone.

4LI: Located at the tip of the angle formed by the first two metacarpals (thumb and index finger bones) when the fingers are spread.

20LI: Located in a hollow at the outside of the nose.

23CV: Located above the Adam's apple.

8Lv: Located on the inner crease of the knee, touching the joint.

67B: Located at the outer corner of the small toenail.

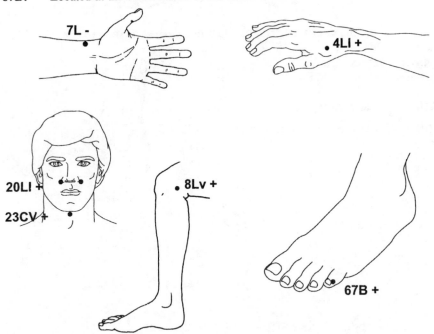

Headaches

Headaches often reflect an energy overload caused by the occasional malfunctioning of one or more digestive organs such as the stomach, the pancreas, the liver, the gall-bladder or the intestines. Here are a few points liable to help get rid of a headache, by improving the functioning of the organs responsible for it.

Aching forehead

Disperse points: Inn-Trang and 4LI.

Inn-Trang: Located on the forehead, between the eyebrows.

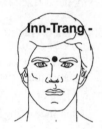

4LI: Located in the angle formed by the first two metacarpals, touching the front of the base of the second metacarpal.

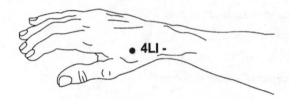

Headache centred at the inner corner of the eye

Disperse point: 62B;
Boost point: 67B.

62B: Located below the lateral malleolus.

67B: Located at the outer corner of the small toenail.

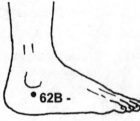

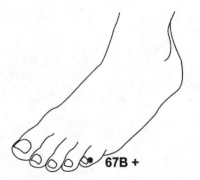

General headache

Disperse points: 4LI, 36S and 3Lv.

4LI: Located at the tip of the angle formed by the first two metacarpals (thumb and index finger) when the fingers are spread.

36S: Located 4 fingerbreadths below the knee, close to the tibia.

3Lv: Located at the summit of the angle formed by the first two metatarsals when the toes are spread.

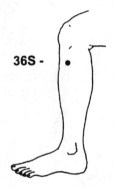
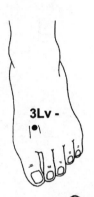

Headache at the back of the head

Disperse points: 3SI, 62B, 44GB and 20GB.

3SI: Located just below the metacarpal/phalanx joint.

62B: Located below the lateral malleolus.

44GB: Located at the outer corner of the fourth toenail.

20GB: Located at the back of the neck, below the occipital protuberances.

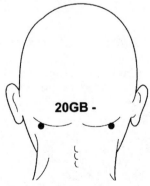
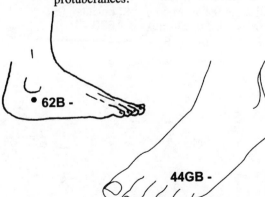

Heart (Bradycardia – abnormally slow heartbeat)

Boost points: 9L and 9H (replace 9H by 5H in winter).

9L: Located in the radial groove, on the wrist crease, before the radial styloid bone.

9H: Located at the inner corner of the little fingernail.

5H: Located on the inside edge of the wrist, in the groove opposite the styloid bone.

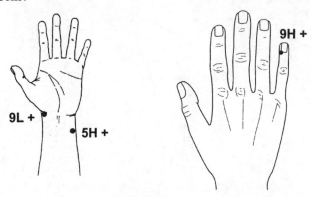

Heart (Pain in the region of)

It is important to consult a cardiologist. As often as not, he will reassure you that the pain is simply due to nerves. The stimulation of energy points can, in many cases, improve the problem and may even get rid of the pain altogether.

Disperse points: 6MH, 4Sp and 21Sp.

Recommended trace elements: Manganese-cobalt and calcium (on alternate days).
Chromium and magnesium are also a good idea (in the afternoon, well outside meal-times, also on alternate days).

Recommended vitamins: B1 (thiamin), C, E.

6MH: Located 3 fingerbreadths above the wrist crease, between the two tendons.

6MH - ●

4Sp: Located in the middle of the inside edge of the foot, on the border between the sole of the foot and the dorsal skin.

21Sp: Located on the side of the thorax, in the sixth intercostal space, ie, in the middle.

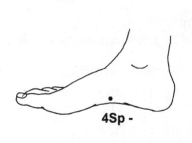

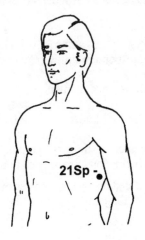

Heart (Palpitations)

It is important to consult a cardiologist. As often as not, he will reassure you that the problem is simply due to nerves. The stimulation of energy points can, in many cases, improve the symptoms and may even get rid of the sensation altogether.

Disperse point: 5H on the right-hand side, then on the left-hand side.

Recommended trace elements: Manganese-cobalt, calcium, chromium, magnesium.

Recommended vitamins: B1 (thiamin), C, E

5H: Located on the inside edge of the wrist, in the groove opposite the small styloid bone.

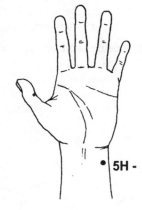

Heart (Tachycardia – abnormally rapid heartbeat)

It is important to consult a cardiologist. As often as not, he will reassure you that the problem is simply due to nerves. The stimulation of energy points can, in many cases, improve the problem and may even get rid of the sensation altogether.

In any season except autumn, disperse point 7H.
In autumn, disperse point 3H.

Recommended trace elements: Manganese-cobalt, calcium, chromium, magnesium.
Recommended vitamins: B1 (thiamin), C, E.

7H: Located on the wrist crease, outside the pisi-form (a small pea-shaped bone in the wrist).

3H: Located on the inner crease of the elbow, level with the joint.

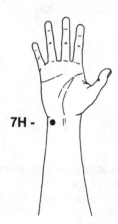

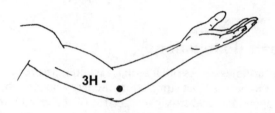

Heartburn

Disperse points: 45S, 36S and 12CV.

45S: Located at the outer corner of the second toenail.

36S: Located 4 fingerbreadths below the knee, between the peroneous longus and the extensor digitorum communis longus.

12CV: Located halfway between the navel and the xiphisternum.

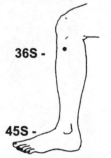

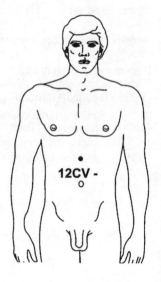

Hot flushes

If the subject's skin is dry, disperse points 20GB and 6Sp.
If the subject is perspiring, disperse points 10B and 6Sp.

20GB: Located at the back of the neck, below the occipital protuberances.

6Sp: Located on the inside of the leg, 4 finger-breadths above the medial malleolus, in a hollow behind the tibia.

10B: Located at the back of the neck, below the occipital protuberances.

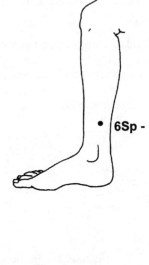

6Sp -

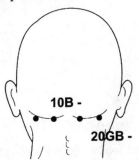

10B -

20GB -

Hypoglycaemia (Abnormally low blood sugar)

Eat vegetables, fruit and wholegrain cereals. Eliminate sugar which encourages the production of insulin by the pancreas and hence a return to the hypoglycaemic state.

Boost points: 36S, 6Sp, 7K and 3SI;
Disperse point: 2Lv;
Boost point: 2Sp.

Recommended trace elements: Magnesium, manganese, zinc.
Recommended vitamins: B6, C.

36S: Located 4 fingerbreadths below the knee, between the peroneous longus and the extensor digitorum communis longus.

36S +

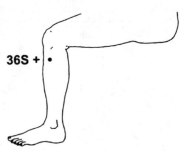

6Sp: Located on the inside of the lower leg, 4 fingerbreadths above the medial malleolus, in a hollow behind the tibia.

7K: Located 2 fingerbreadths above the medial malleolus, in front of the Achilles' tendon.

3SI: Located just after the metacarpal/phalanx joint.

2Lv: Located in between the first two toes.

2Sp: Located on the inside of the foot, just before the big toe joint.

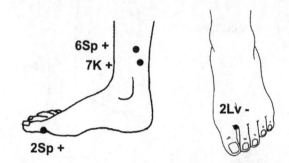

Immune defences

To stimulate the immune defences, the following points are ideal:

Boost points: 6Sp, 23B, 7K, 4GV, 8Lv, 18B, 38B and 9L.

6Sp: Located on the inside of the leg, 4 fingerbreadths above the medial malleolus, in a hollow behind the tibia.

23B: Located level with the second and third lumbar vertebrae.

7K: Located 2 fingerbreadths above the medial malleolus, in front of the Achilles' tendon.

4GV: Located in the hollow of the back, level with the kidneys, between the second and third lumbar vertebrae.

8Lv: Located on the inner crease of the knee, touching the joint.

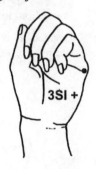

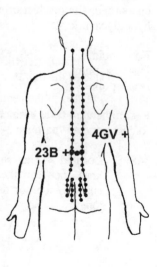

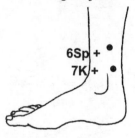

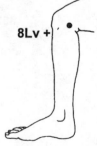

18B: Located level with the ninth and tenth dorsal vertebrae.

38B: Located on the inner edge of the shoulder-blade.

9L: Located in the radial groove, on the wrist crease, ie, before the radial styloid bone.

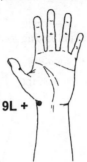

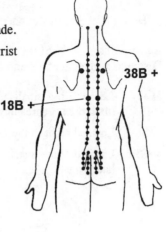

38B +

18B +

9L +

Incontinence (Urinary)

Boost points: 7K, 23B, 25GB and 64B.

Recommended trace element: Copper-gold-silver.

7K: Located 2 fingerbreadths above the medial malleolus, in front of the Achilles' tendon.

23B: Located level with the second and third lumbar vertebrae, 2 fingerbreadths to either side of the spine.

25GB: Located at the tip of the twelfth rib, which is the floating rib whose point can be seen on the side of the thorax.

64B: Located in the centre of the outer edge of the foot, behind the joint of the fifth metatarsal.

23B +

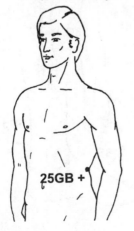

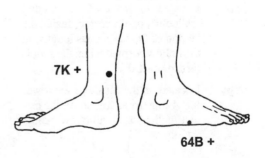

7K +

64B +

25GB +

Itching

Here are the points connected with itching and which are liable to soothe it:

Boost point: 5Lv;
Disperse points: 54B and 40GB.

5Lv: Located in a small hollow on the inner side of the tibia, 5 fingerbreadths above the medial malleolus.

54B: Located right in the middle of the back of the knee.

40GB: Located at the instep, in a hollow just in front of the lateral malleolus.

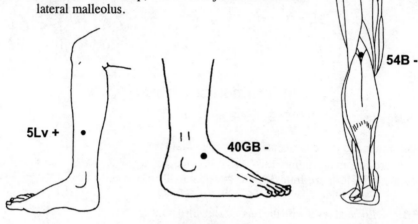

Legs (Tired)

I recommend you begin by stimulating the Tae Mo EV (page 114), particularly if you are suffering from horizontal back pain in the lumbar region or from wind. Alternatively, stimulate the Tchrong Mo EV (page 118), particularly if you suffer from hormone, gynaecological or menstrual disorders.

Disperse points: 5Sp, 6Sp and 32S;
Boost points: 1Lv and 2Lv;
Disperse point: 3Lv.

5Sp: Located in front of the medial malleolus, on the instep, inside the tendon of the peroneous longus, in the hollow formed when the foot is turned inwards.

6Sp: Located on the inside of the lower leg, 4 fingerbreadths above the medial malleolus, in a hollow behind the tibia.

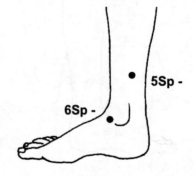

32S: Located in the middle of the front of the thigh.

1Lv: Located at the outer side of the big toenail.

2Lv: Located in between the first two toes.

3Lv: Located at the tip of the angle formed by the first two metatarsals when the toes are spread.

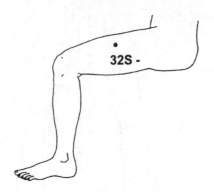

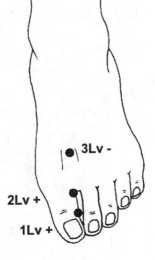

Liver (Sluggish)

There are many points that can assist the liver's functioning when they are stimulated. Here are four that will no doubt surprise you by their effectiveness:

Boost points: 3Lv, 8Lv, 14Lv and 18B.

3Lv: Located at the tip of the angle formed by the first two metatarsals when the toes are spread.

8Lv: Located on the inside of the crease formed when the knee is bent, touching the joint.

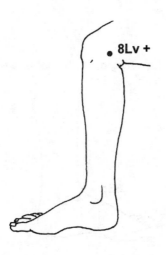

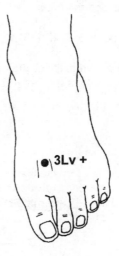

14Lv: Located between the sixth and seventh ribs, directly below the nipple.

18B: Located level with the ninth and tenth dorsal vertebrae.

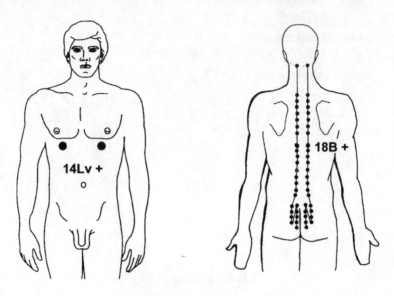

Liver disorders

Eat: Fruit, vegetables, wholegrain cereals.
                                  Cold-pressed virgin vegetable oils.
Avoid: Animal fats, alcohol, coffee, tobacco.
Drink: Freshly squeezed lemon juice.
Recommended infusion: Rosemary.
Recommended trace element: Zinc.
Recommended plant: Fumeterre.
Recommended vitamins: B6, C.

Disperse points: 4Sp, 3Lv, 8Lv and 14Lv.

4Sp: Located in the centre of the inside edge of the foot, on the border between the sole of the foot and the dorsal skin.

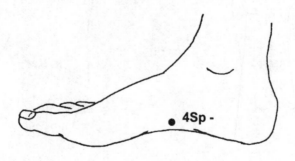

3Lv: Located on the foot, at the tip of the angle formed when the first two metatarsals are spread, touching the big toe bone.

8Lv: Located on the inside of the crease behind the knee, touching the joint.

14Lv: Located between the sixth and seventh ribs, directly below the nipple.

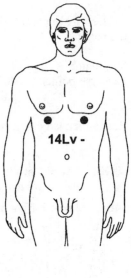
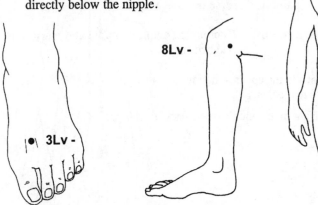

Lower abdomen (Spasms in the)

Disperse points: 6MH and 9Sp.

6MH: Located 3 fingerbreadths above the wrist crease, between the two tendons.

9Sp: Located below the outside of the knee, touching the joint.

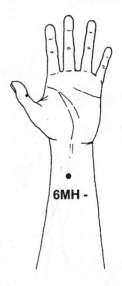
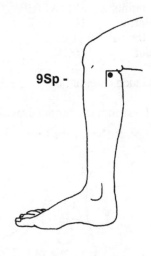

Lumbago

Here are the points that work wonders in the case of lumbago spreading round the back:

Stimulate: Tae Mo EV (page 109);
Disperse points: 40GB and 54B. In the event of any points remaining
                  painful, disperse these as well.

Recommended essential oils: Camomile complex, thyme and marjoram
                              (rubbed in).

40GB: Located at the instep, in a hollow just in front of
            the lateral malleolus.

54B: Located right in the middle of the back of the knee.

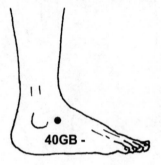

Lumbago (Along the spine)

Disperse points: 3SI and 62B;
Boost point: 1GV;
Disperse the painful points;
Boost point: 26GV.

Recommended essential oil: Juniper, thyme (rubbed in).

3SI: Located just after the metacarpal/phalanx joint.

62B: Located below the lateral malleolus.

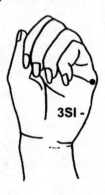

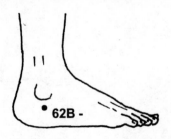

1GV: Located on the tip of the coccyx.

26GV: Located in the hollow just below the nose.

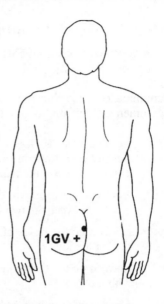

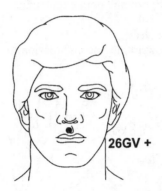

26GV +

1GV +

Lumbago (Vertical pain)

If the pain is not exactly along the spine, but slightly to either side of the vertebral column, here are the points that should be stimulated in the following order:

Disperse points: 62B, 3SI and 54B;
Boost point: 67B.

62B: Located below the lateral malleolus.

3SI: Located just after the metacarpal/phalanx joint

54B: Located right in the middle of the back of the knee.

67B: Located at the outer corner of the small toenail.

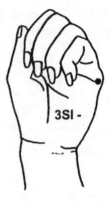

3SI -

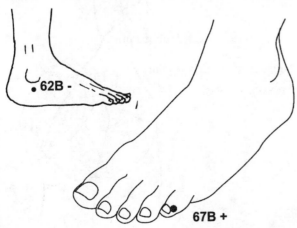

62B -

67B +

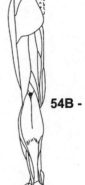

54B -

Memory (To stimulate)

Disperse points: 7L and 6MH;
Boost points: 2Sp, 3H, 20GV and 11LI.

Recommended trace elements: Magnesium, phosphorus, zinc.
Recommended vitamin: B1.

7L: Located in the radial groove where you can feel the pulse, 3 fingerbreadths above the wrist crease, ie, above the radial styloid.

6MH: Located 3 fingerbreadths above the wrist crease, between the two tendons.

2Sp: Located on the inside of the foot, just before the big toe joint.

3H: Located on the crease inside the elbow, level with the joint.

20GV: Located on the top of the head, on a line drawn between the tops of the ears.

11LI: Located at the outermost point of the elbow crease.

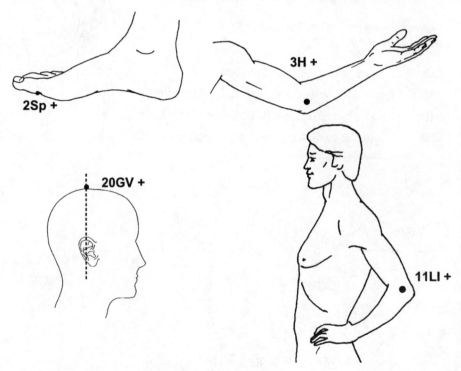

Migraine

The pain is centred above the eyes, level with the eyebrows, and very often at a specific point which can be in the centre. The cause is often linked with digestive disorders, particularly in connection with the liver and the gall-bladder (even if the latter has been surgically removed).

Avoid: Alcohol, coffee, chocolate.
Eat: Cold-pressed virgin vegetable oils, lemon.

Disperse points: 7L, 40GB, 3Lv and 20GB.

7L: Located in the radial groove where you can feel the pulse, 3 fingerbreadths above the wrist crease, ie, above the radial styloid.

40GB: Located at the top of the foot, in a hollow just in front of the lateral malleolus.

3Lv: Located on the foot, at the tip of the angle formed by the first two metatarsals when the toes are spread, touching the big toe bone.

20GB: Located at the back of the neck, below the occipital protuberances.

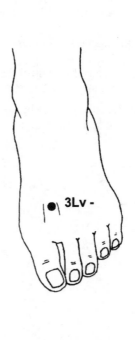

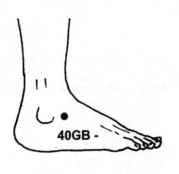

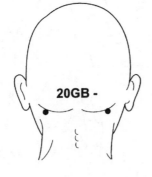

Mouth (Bitter taste upon waking)

Disperse points: 38GB, 34GB and 36S.

Recommended essential oils: Mint (one drop on the tongue after meals), rosemary (rubbed into the skin in the region of the liver and gall-bladder).

38GB: Located 4 fingerbreadths above the lateral malleolus, in a small hollow on the front of the fibula.

34GB: Located below the outside of the knee, below the head of the fibula, the small bony bump one can feel just below the knee, slightly to the rear.

36S: Located 4 fingerbreadths below the knee, close to the tibia.

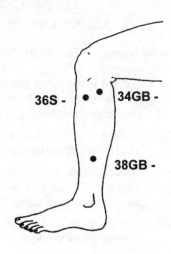

Mouth ulcers

Boost points: 3Lv and 12CV;
Disperse points: 1LI, 2LI and 4LI.

Recommended trace element: Magnesium.

3Lv: Located at the tip of the angle formed by the first two metatarsals when the toes are spread.

12CV: Located halfway between the navel and the xiphisternum.

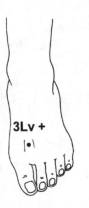

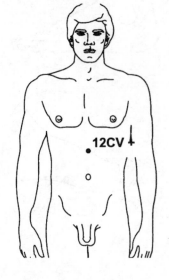

1LI: Located at the inner corner of the index fingernail.

2LI: Located just below the metacarpal/phalanx joint, on the inside of the index finger.

4LI: Located in the angle formed by the first two metacarpals, touching the front of the second metacarpal.

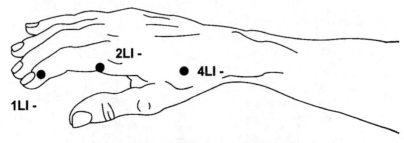

Mucus (To dry up mucus)

Boost point: 2Sp;
Disperse points: 40S and 36S;
Boost points: 10L and 5Sp.

2Sp: Located on the inside of the foot, just before the big toe joint.

40S: Located almost halfway up the lower leg, 2 fingerbreadths outside the tibial ridge, slightly above and to the side of point 39S, between the muscles and in front of the fibula.

36S: Located 4 fingerbreadths below the knee, between the peroneous longus and the extensor digitorum communis longus.

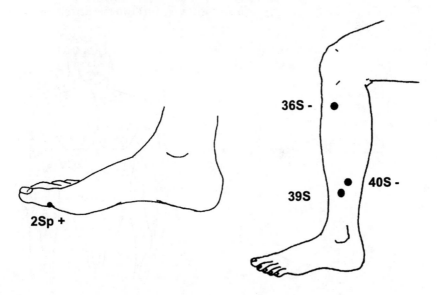

10L: Located right in the centre of the first metacarpal, on the thenar eminence, level with the anchorage point of the thumb's abductor muscle.

5Sp: Located in front of the medial malleolus, at the instep, inside the tendon of the peroneous longus, in the hollow formed when the foot is turned inwards.

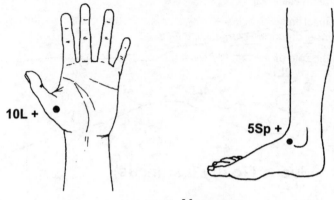

Nausea

Disperse points: 40GB, 21K and 36S.

40GB: Located at the instep, in a hollow in front of the lateral malleolus.

21K: Located on the thorax, 2 fingerbreadths outside the median line, level with the tip of the xiphisternum.

36S: Located 4 fingerbreadths below the knee, between the peroneous longus and the extensor digitorum communis longus.

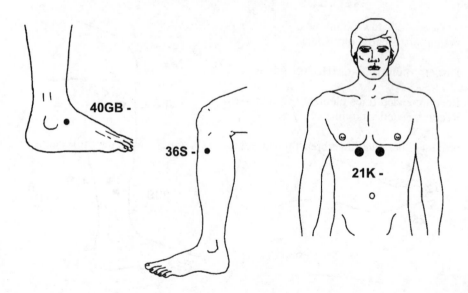

Nerves (An attack of)

Boost points: 5H, 36S and 1K.

5H: Located on the inside of the wrist, in a small groove opposite the styloid bone.

36S: Located 4 fingerbreadths below the knee, between the peroneous longus and the extensor digitorum communis longus.

1K: Located on the sole of the foot, between the two muscle masses.

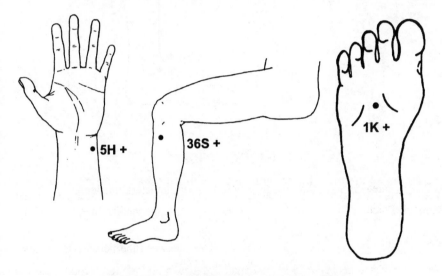

Nervous, excitable personality

Here are a few points whose soothing and balancing action on the nervous system are greatly appreciated:

Disperse points: 6MH, 36S and 3Lv.

Recommended trace element: Magnesium.
Recommended vitamin: B.

6MH: Located 3 fingerbreadths above the wrist crease, between the two tendons.

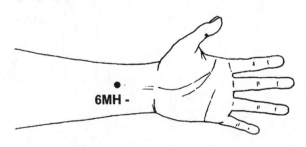

36S: Located 4 fingerbreadths below the knee, between the peroneous longus and the extensor digitorum communis longus.

3Lv: Located on the foot, at the tip of the angle formed by the first two metatarsals when the toes are spread, touching the big toe bone.

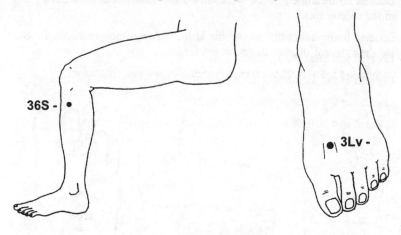

Nightmares

Nightmares are often linked with digestive disorders and worries; so it is not at all surprising to discover that the anti-nightmare point is situated on the Stomach PM.

Boost point: 44S.

44S: Located between the second and third toes, alongside the second toe.

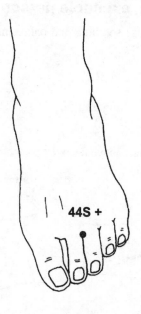

Nose (Blocked)

Disperse points: 4LI, 20LI, 66B, 10B, 1B and 24CV.

4LI: Located in the angle formed by the first two metacarpals, touching the base of the second metacarpal.

20LI: Located in the hollow at the outside of the base of the nose.

66B: Located just after the small toe joint.

10B: Located at the back of the neck, below the occipital protuberances.

1B: Located at the inner corner of the eye.

24CV: Located in a hollow between the tip of the chin and the lower lip.

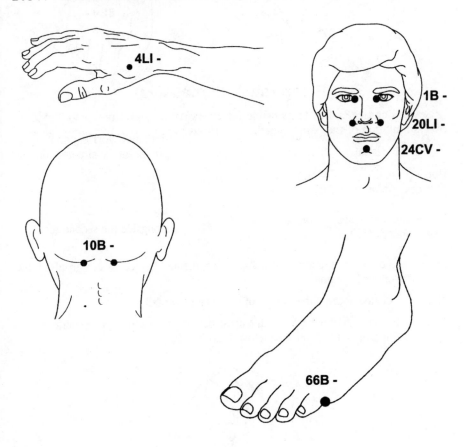

Nose (Runny)

Boost points: 67B and 1LI.

67B: Located at the outer corner of the small toenail.

1LI: Located at the inner corner of the index finger, alongside the thumb.

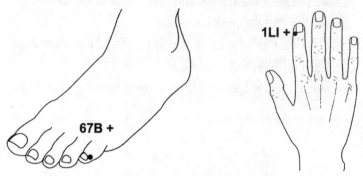

Perspiration (Excessive)

Several causes can be responsible for excessive perspiration: weak kidneys, overstimulation of the parasympathetic nervous system, lack of vigour, general weakness.

Boost points: 7K and 1SI;
Disperse point: 10B.

Recommended trace element: Zinc.
Recommended vitamin: E.

7K: Located 2 fingerbreadths above the medial malleolus, in front of the Achilles' tendon.

1SI: Located at the outer corner of the little fingernail.

10B: Located at the back of the neck below the occipital protuberances, 2 fingerbreadths from the median line.

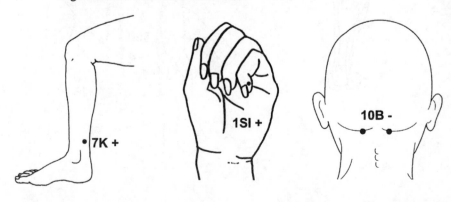

Prostate gland disorders

Disperse points: 6K, 4Sp, 54B and 64B;
Boost points: 31B and 32B.

6K: Located below the medial malleolus.

4Sp: Located on the inside of the foot, on the border between the sole of the foot and the dorsal skin.

54B: Located right in the middle of the back of the knee.

64B: Located in the centre of the outside edge of the foot, in front of the small toe joint.

31B: Located in the first sacral hollow.

32B: Located in the second sacral hollow.

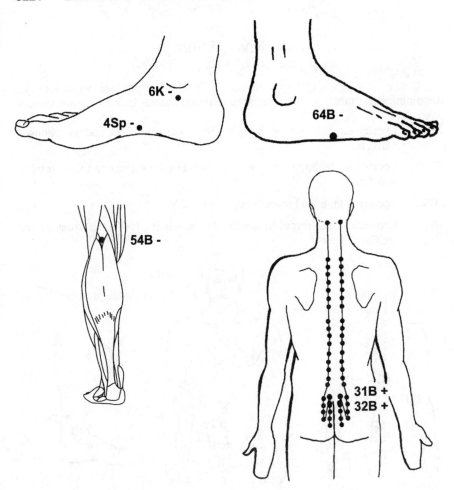

School marks (To improve them)

The stimulation of this point aids concentration and renders the mind more capable of synthesis and solving mathematical problems.

Boost point: 2Sp.

2Sp: Located on the inside of the foot, just before the big toe joint.

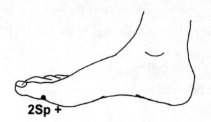

Sex drive (Waning)

Boost points: 23B, 4GV, 5CV and 7K.

Recommended plants: Ginseng, savory.

23B: Located on either side of the spine, level with the second and third lumbar vertebrae.

4GV: Located in the hollow of the back, between the second and third lumbar vertebrae.

5CV: Located 1 thumb's breadth above point 4CV.

7K: Located 2 fingerbreadths above the medial malleolus, in front of the Achilles' tendon.

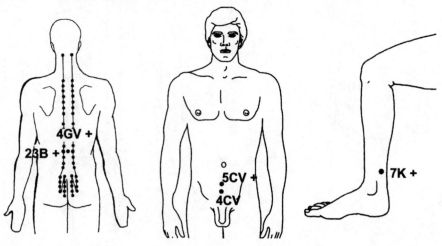

Shoulder
(Pain at the back or on the top of the shoulder)

Disperse points: 5TH and 41GB;
Boost points: 1TH and 1SI;
Disperse points: 15TH, 10SI, 11SI and 20GV.

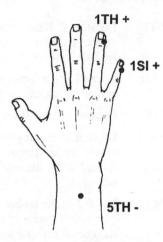

5TH: Located 2 fingerbreadths above the crease on the back of the wrist, between the two bones of the forearm.

41GB: Located at the tip of the angle formed by the last two metatarsals.

1TH: Located at the corner of the fourth fingernail, alongside the little finger.

1SI: Located at the outer corner of the little fingernail.

15TH: Located behind the shoulder, on the upper side of the trapezius muscle, close to the top of the inner edge of the shoulder-blade, level with the first dorsal vertebra.

10SI: Located below the ridge of the shoulder-blade, in the groove of the infraspinous.

11SI: Located in the centre of the infraspinous groove, ie, almost in the middle of the shoulder-blade.

20GV: Located on the top of the skull, on a line which would join the tops of the ears.

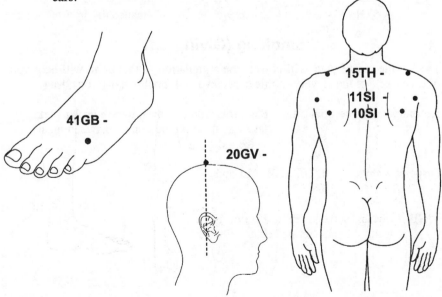

Shoulder
(Pain on the outer side of the front of the shoulder)

Disperse point: 5TH;
Boost points: 1LI and 11L;
Disperse points: 15LI and 2L.

5TH: Located 2 fingerbreadths above the crease on the back of the wrist, between the two bones of the forearm.

1LI: Located at the corner of the index fingernail, alongside the thumb.

11L: Located at the corner of the thumbnail.

15LI: Located at the angle of the shoulder, below the acromion, in the hollow formed when the arm is stretched out sideways.

2L: Located in the hollow below the clavicle, which becomes deeper when the shoulder is brought forward.

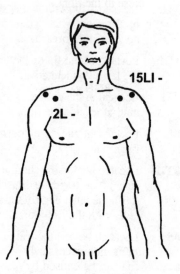

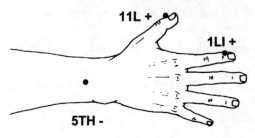

Smoking (Giving up)

With the aid of your will-power, the stimulation of this point will help you free yourself of the slavery to this expensive and terribly dangerous drug.

Recommended essential oil: Sassafras (rub one drop into the solar plexus; take one drop on the tongue between meals, twice a day).

Disperse points: 40GB, 8GB, 4LI and 36S.

40GB: Located at the instep, in a hollow in front of the lateral malleolus.

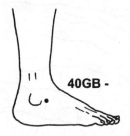

8GB: Located in a hollow 2 fingerbreadths above the uppermost tip of the ear.

4LI: Located at the tip of the angle formed by the first two metacarpals (thumb and index finger bones) when the fingers are spread.

36S: Located 4 fingerbreadths below the knee, close to the tibia.

36S -

8GB -

4LI -

Sneezing fits

Sneezing is not necessarily a sign that you are going to develop a cold. Sneezing fits can be caused by an allergic reaction or by a chronic runny nose.

Disperse points: 5L, 4LI, 20LI and 1B;
Boost point: 8Lv.

Recommended trace elements: Manganese-copper-magnesium-lithium, zinc.
Recommended vitamin: C.

5L: Located in the hollow of the elbow crease, outside the biceps tendon.

4LI: Located at the tip of the angle formed by the first two metacarpals (the thumb and index finger bones) when the fingers are spread.

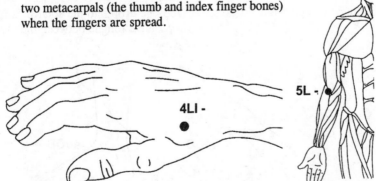

5L -

4LI -

20LI: Located in a hollow next to the bottom of the nose.

1B: Located at the inner corner of the eye.

8Lv: Located on the inside of the crease behind the knee, touching the joint.

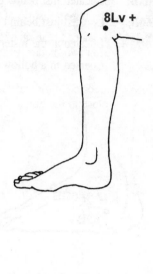

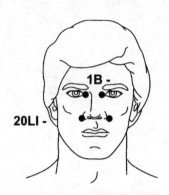

Sprain (On the outer side of the ankle)

In the case of a serious sprain, it is important to have an X-ray done to make sure nothing is broken.

Here are the points that will help the joint recover its full range of movement in a very short time, as long as it is only a simple sprain and it is treated rapidly. Two sessions per day for two or three days, if necessary.

Boost points: 67B and 44GB on both sides;
Disperse points: 62B, 60B and 40GB on the same side as the sprain;
Boost point: 2S on the same side as the sprain.

67B: Located at the outer corner of the small toenail.

44GB: Located at the outer corner of the fourth toenail.

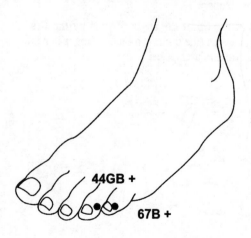

62B: Located just below the lateral malleolus.

60B: Located just behind the lateral malleolus.

40GB: Located at the instep, in a hollow just in front of the lateral malleolus.

2S: Located in a hollow just below point 1S.

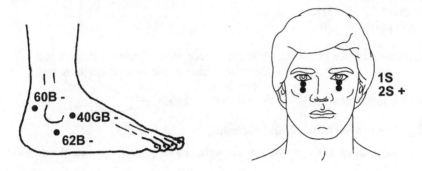

Stress

Disperse points: 6MH, 36S and 17CV;
Boost point: 6CV.

6MH: Located 3 fingerbreadths above the wrist crease, between the two tendons.

36S: Located 4 fingerbreadths below the knee, between the peroneous longus and the extensor digitorum communis longus.

17CV: Located on the sternum, between the breasts.

6CV: Located 2 fingerbreadths below the navel.

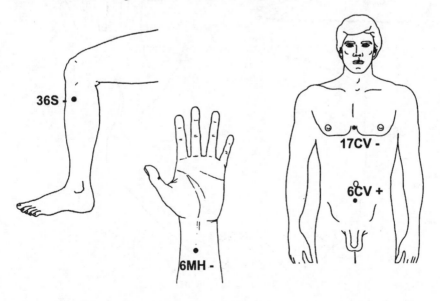

Stuttering

Stuttering can be reduced by calming the subject's nervousness and encouraging their inner control. Here are a few points that can help:

Disperse point: 62B;
Boost point: 5H;
Disperse point: 36S.

Recommended trace elements: Manganese-copper-magnesium-lithium and zinc (first thing in the morning, alternating every day).
Recommended vitamins: B (brewer's yeast), C .

62B: Located below the lateral malleolus.

5H: Located on the inner side of the wrist, in the groove opposite the styloid bone.

36S: Located 4 fingerbreadths below the knee, close to the tibia.

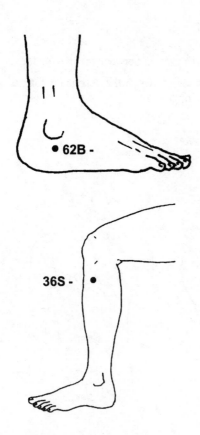

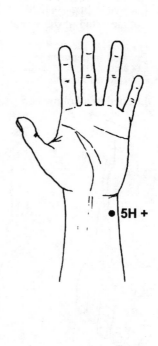

Sunburn

It is not prudent to expose the skin to the sun for long periods. Exposure must be gradual and for short periods only, otherwise sunburn requiring hospital treatment could occur.

In the case of minor sunburn, or other slight burns, the stimulation of this point is often helpful:

Disperse point: 7L.

7L: Located in the radial groove where one can feel the pulse, 3 fingerbreadths above the crease formed when the wrist is bent, ie, above the radial styloid bone.

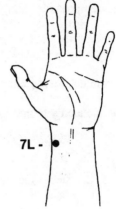

Thirst (Excessive)

Disperse point: 2LV;
Boost point: 1K;
Disperse point: 24CV.

2Lv: Located in between the first two toes.

1K: Located on the sole of the foot, between the two muscle masses.

24CV: Located in a hollow between the tip of the chin and the lower lip.

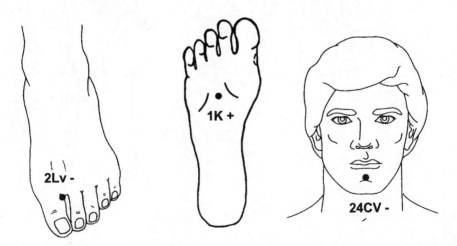

Throat (Sore)

Sore throats should be treated as soon as the first symptoms are felt because they can easily degenerate into influenza, sinusitis or other, more serious diseases such as severe rheumatic fever which 'licks the joints but bites the heart' – meaning that the joints are only affected in passing, for a short while, but serious cardiac infections can last forever. It is important to get rid of a sore throat as quickly as possible. Gargles and mouthwashes made of salty water and lemon juice are ideal.

Boost points: 1LI, 9L, 11L, 7K, 22CV and 23CV.

Recommended trace elements: Iodine, manganese-copper-magnesium-lithium, sulphur.

Recommended vitamin: C.

1LI: Located at the inner corner of the index fingernail, alongside the thumb.

9L: Located in the radial groove, on the wrist crease, ie, before the radial styloid.

11L: Located at the corner of the thumbnail.

7K: Located 2 fingerbreadths above the medial malleolus, in front of the Achilles' tendon.

22CV: Located in the hollow above the fork in the sternum.

23CV: Located above the Adam's apple.

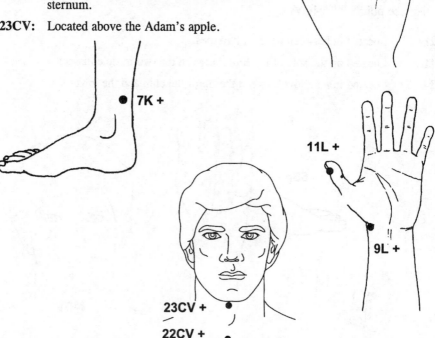

Toe (Painful big toe)

The most common and the most painful type of pain affecting the big toe is undoubtedly gout. The big toe joint becomes swollen, red, hot and extremely painful.

A healthy diet is a must: eliminate alcohol, pork and sugar. Eat vegetables, salads, fruit and wholegrain cereals.

Recommended decoction: Linden, orthosyphon.
Recommended essential oil: Juniper.
Recommended trace elements: Iodine, magnesium, sulphur, zinc.
Recommended vitamins: B15, C.

Disperse points: 4Sp, 5Sp and 3Lv.

4Sp: Located in the middle of the inside edge of the foot, on the border between the sole of the foot and the dorsal skin.

5Sp: Located in front of the medial malleolus, at the instep, inside the tendon of the peroneous longus, in the hollow formed when the foot is turned inwards.

3Lv: Located on the upper side of the foot, at the tip of the angle formed when the first two metatarsals are spread, touching the big toe bone.

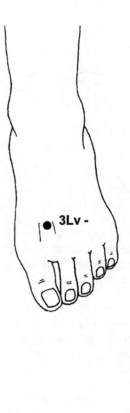

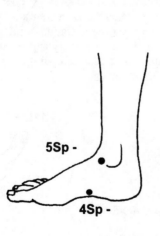

Toothache

Our teeth are mainly connected with the Large intestine and the Stomach meridians. Here are two points that can help relieve toothache, but which obviously cannot replace a dentist:

Disperse point: 4LI;
Boost point: 45S.

4LI: Located in the angle formed by the first two metacarpals, touching the base of the second metacarpal.

45S: Located at the outer corner of the second toenail.

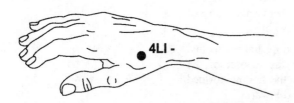

Urination (Excessive)

Urinating too often can be a sign of an energy deficiency in the kidneys and the adrenal glands, and it is therefore likely that the body's defences will be diminished. In this case, it is important to boost the kidneys' energy, which will in turn stimulate the immune defence system and encourage better selective filtering and elimination of waste, thus avoiding letting minerals escape.

This stimulation of kidney energy will also be greatly appreciated by subjects suffering from rheumatism, exhaustion and a lack of courage. It is also vital to people who have trouble making up their minds.

Boost points: 23B and 64B.
In winter, boost points 7K and 67B.
In spring, boost points 10K and 66B.
In summer, boost point 1K.
In autumn, boost points 3K and 54B.

Recommended essential oil: Savory.
Recommended trace elements: Copper-gold-silver, silica.

23B: Located level with the second and third lumbar vertebrae, 2 fingerbreadths from the median line.

64B: Located in the centre of the outside of the foot, behind the joint of the fifth metatarsal.

7K: Located 2 fingerbreadths above the lateral malleolus, in front of the Achilles' tendon.

67B: Located at the outer corner of the small toenail.

10K: Located in the crease behind the knee.

66B: Located just above the small toe joint.

1K: Located on the sole of the foot, between the two muscle masses.

3K: Located just behind the medial malleolus.

54B: Located right in the middle of the back of the knee.

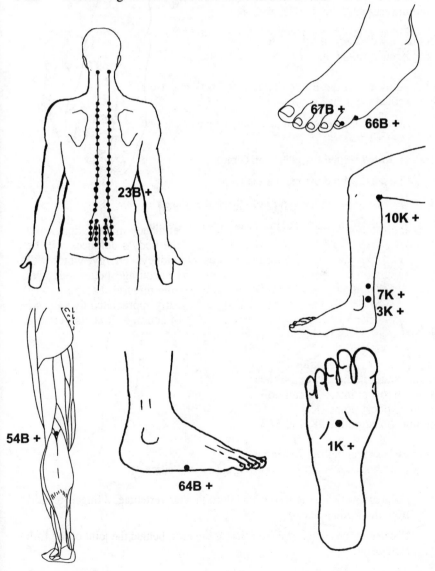

Urination (Insufficient)

Contrary to popular belief, it is not a good sign to urinate too often, ie, more than six times a day and to go to the toilet during the night. The water thus evacuated is likely to rinse away useful mineral salts, leading to decalcification. But in some cases, it is important to activate insufficient urination. If you do not urinate often enough, here are the points that will help you:

In winter, disperse points 65B and 1K.
In spring, disperse points 60B and 3K.
In summer, disperse points 54B and 3K.
In autumn, disperse points 64B and 1K.

Recommended essential oil: Juniper.
Recommended infusion: Cherry stalks.

65B: Located on the inside of the foot, just behind the small toe joint.

1K: Located on the sole of the foot, between the two muscle masses.

60B: Located behind the lateral malleolus.

3K: Located behind the medial malleolus.

54B: Located right in the centre of the back of the knee.

64B: Located in the middle of the outside edge of the foot.

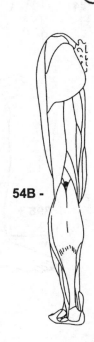

1K -

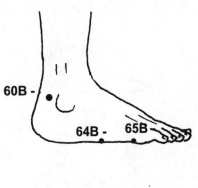

60B -

64B -   65B -

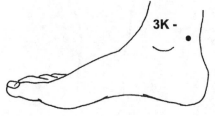

3K -

54B -

Verrucas

As well as stimulating the following points, I recommend that you also drink a glass of the following preparation, first thing every morning for three weeks: stir 20 g of magnesium chloride into a litre of pure water.

It is not necessary to take all the natural medication listed below. Sometimes, the stimulation of the given points, twice a day for 4 to 7 days, is enough to get rid of a verruca. However, it is advisable to combine homoeopathy and trace elements – particularly magnesium – as a basic treatment and thus avoid the problem recurring. As for lavender oil, it is an antiseptic which promotes the regeneration of tissues.

Recommended trace elements: Magnesium, silica, zinc.
Recommended homoeopathy: Thuya 4CH (3 granules 3 times a day for 10
                             days), Nitricum Acidum 4CH (3 granules 3
                             times a day for 10 days).
Recommended essential oil: Lavender.
Recommended tincture: Thuya (3 drops applied directly to the verruca).
Recommended vitamins: E, F (cold-pressed virgin vegetable oils).

Boost point: 39S.
Disperse all the points situated around and on the verruca, using the Electronic Pointer (page 12).

39S: Located on the outside of the leg, 4 fingerbreadths above the lateral malleolus.

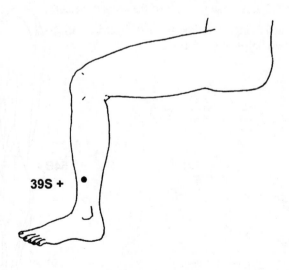

39S +

Voice loss

Boost points: 4LI, 11L and 9S.

4LI: Located in the angle formed by the first two metacarpals, touching the base of the second metacarpal.

11L: Located at the corner of the thumbnail.

9S: Located on the front edge of the sterno-cleidomastoid muscle, on the carotid artery.

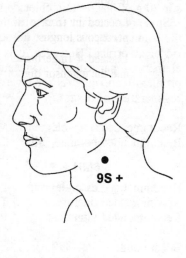

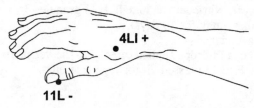

Wind

In typical yang subjects, disperse points 41GB, 45S and 5TH.
In typical yin subjects, boost points 4Sp, 6MH, 5Sp and 36S.

41GB: Located at the tip of the angle formed by the last two metatarsals.

45S: Located at the outer corner of the second toenail.

5TH: Located 2 fingerbreadths above the crease on the back of the wrist, between the two bones in the forearm.

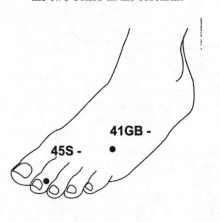

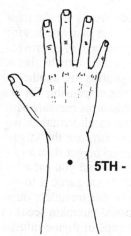

4Sp: Located in the centre of the inside of the foot, on the border between the sole of the foot and the dorsal skin.

6MH: Located 3 fingerbreadths above the inner wrist crease, between the two tendons.

5Sp: Located in front of the medial malleolus, just inside the tendon of the peroneous longus, in the hollow formed when the foot is turned inwards.

36S: Located 4 fingerbreadths below the knee, between the peroneous longus and the extensor digitorum communis longus.

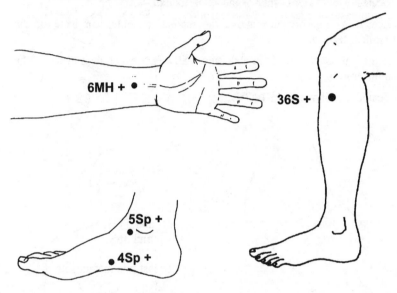

Worms

Threadworms are the most common type of worms that infest the intestines. They are less than one centimetre long, and lay their eggs around the anus which causes itching. Try to prevent children scratching the area and then putting their fingers in their mouths, because this causes reinfection.

Whipworms are another sort of intestinal parasite, less than 5 cm long but sometimes responsible for wasting diarrhoea, headaches and dizziness.

Roundworms measure between 10 and 20 cm and resemble earthworms. They can cause much irritation, nausea and even abdominal pain.

Tapeworms are the largest type of intestinal parasite. Make sure the head, which is no bigger than a pinhead, is completely expelled.

I recommend you eat a lot of garlic (several cloves a day, if possible). The best way to eat garlic is to swallow the cloves whole, first thing in the morning. Complete this treatment during the daytime by eating 60 to 100 g of blanched and crushed pumpkin seeds every day, mixed with a spoonful of honey. Drink several cups of thyme infusion, particularly first thing in the morning with the garlic. Cabbage juice, carrot juice and lemon juice are also recommended.

Stimulate the following points on the day before, during and after the new moon:

Boost points: 67B, 7K, 12CV and 13CV.
On the third day of the treatment, drink a purgative made of linseed oil (30 g).

Recommended essential oils: Clove, thyme (rubbed into the lower back).
Recommended trace element: Sulphur.

67B: Located at the outer corner of the small toenail.

7K: Located 2 fingerbreadths above the medial malleolus, in front of the Achilles' tendon.

12CV: Located in the centre of the abdomen, halfway between the navel and the xiphisternum.

13CV: Located just above point 12CV.

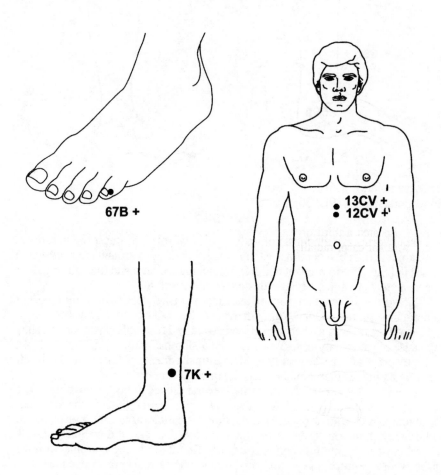

Wounds (Healing)

The following points accelerate the healing of wounds, sometimes with spectacular results.

Boost points: 6Sp and 39GB.

Recommended trace elements: Magnesium, zinc.
Recommended vitamin: B5 (pantothenic acid).

6Sp: Located on the inside of the leg, 4 fingerbreadths above the medial malleolus, in a hollow behind the tibia.

39GB: Located 2 fingerbreadths above the lateral malleolus, on the fibula.

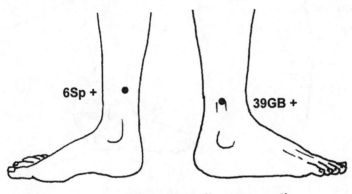

Yawning (Incessant)

Disperse point: 6LI;
Boost points: 9L, 36S and 6Sp.

6LI: Located a third of the way up the outside of the forearm, in front of the flexor carpi radialis brevis, 4 fingerbreadths above point 5LI.

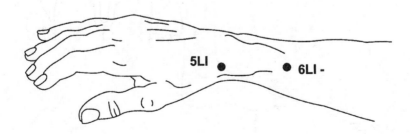

9L: Located in the radial groove, on the wrist crease, ie, above the radial styloid (a bone in the wrist).

36S: Located 4 fingerbreadths below the knee, close to the tibia.

6Sp: Located on the inside of the lower leg, 4 fingerbreadths above the medial malleolus, in a hollow behind the tibia.

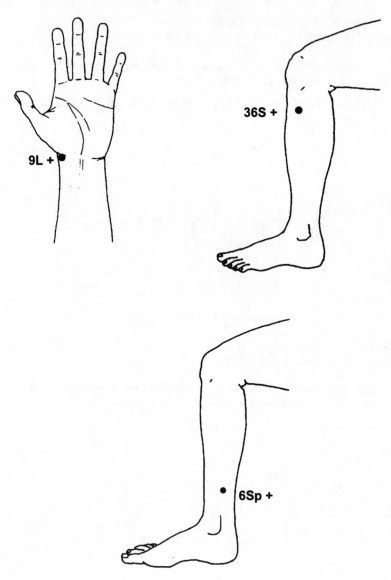